PRAISE

"Dr. Sullivan understands firefighters, the stressors we face, and the traps we fall into. *Cover My Six* is a practical guide to navigating mental health in our profession. It is explicitly written for firefighters by someone who understands how we think and respond to stressors. This is a book you will use yourself and share with your peers."

—CARL E., career Captain, 25 years

"After 8 years of marriage and 13 years in fire service, it is evident I have changed emotionally due to the stressors and experiences from work. As first responders, we go through events and see things a lot of individuals will never experience in their lives. This method has opened my wife's eyes to things I don't talk about at home, and why I may not talk about certain events with her. *Cover My Six* has left us with the tools to navigate these areas. I hope other counselors will follow in Lea's footsteps, as I believe this will help MANY responders move forward."

—DERIC & LISA K., career Lieutenant FF/EMT, 13 years

"*Cover My Six* speaks our language! Dr. Lea gets what it means to be a firefighter—the grit, the sacrifice, and the weight we carry. This book isn't just about surviving the job; it's about thriving in it. A must-read for every firefighter who wants to take care of their crew and themselves."

—RYAN L., military family and career Probationary FF/EMT

"*Cover My Six* is a guide that's not just informative—it's culturally competent and empowering. Lea speaks to the fire service with both authority and care, which is rare. This book will resonate deeply with both the tough, skeptical firefighters and the ones actively seeking mental wellness. If this book had existed when I started, it would've changed how I approached stress, trauma, and recovery."

—RYAN C., career Captain FF/PM, 19 years

"As first responders, we are highly trained to help others, to fix emergencies, and to stay strong in the face of crisis. But that same training can make it difficult to recognize when we need to help ourselves—when the weight of the job and years of trauma begin to take a toll. *Cover My Six* is the resource we've been missing. It helps first responders recognize when they may be struggling, understand the support available, and navigate their mental health journey."

—DANIELLE S., career FF/PM and second-generation first responder

"I can confidently say that Lea has an unparalleled understanding of the fire service and the challenges that frontline members face. Her insights in *Cover My Six* not only are deeply empathetic but also resonate profoundly with the realities of our profession."

—JOHN B., career Chaplain, 15 years,
and father of two law enforcement officers

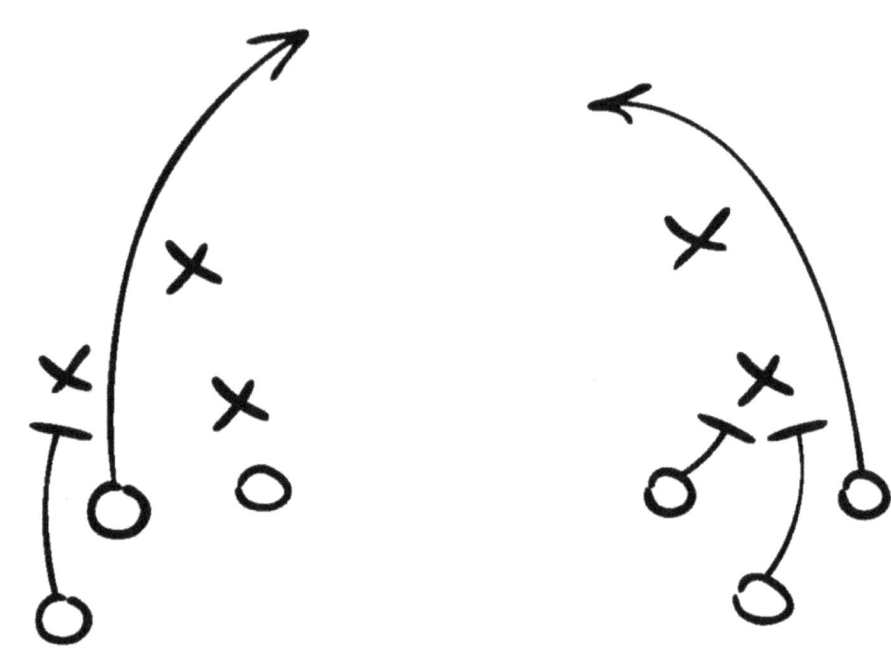

COVER MY SIX
The Playbook

Also By Lea Sullivan, PhD, LMHC, Ret. Chaplain

Cover My Six: A Comprehensive Guide to Firefighter Care

Frequent contributing author to *Firefighter Nation* magazine

COVER MY SIX
The Playbook

Twelve Essential Trainings
for Firefighter Peer Support

Lea Sullivan, PhD, LMHC, Ret. Chaplain

STRONG RED LINE

PUBLICATIONS

STRONG RED LINE

PUBLICATIONS

For information about special discounts for bulk purchases or author interviews, appearances, and speaking engagements, please contact:

https://DrLeaSullivan.com/

First Edition

ISBN spiral bound: 979-8-9990118-4-8
ISBN hardcover: 979-8-9990118-5-5
ISBN softcover: 979-8-9990118-6-2
ISBN ebook: 979-8-9990118-7-9

Library of Congress: <<>>

Cover design by Lea Sullivan
Page Design & Produced by Rodney Miles

Look, if cauliflower
can become pizza...
then you, my friend,
can be anything.[1]

---

[1] The quote, "Look, if cauliflower can become pizza... then you, my friend, can be anything," is a motivational phrase popularized by Amy Lacy, the founder of Cauliflower Foods, who developed and marketed a cauliflower pizza crust. While the exact origin of the phrase isn't definitive, Lacy often uses it to inspire people about the potential for transformation and overcoming challenges, drawing a parallel to how cauliflower itself was transformed into a popular food product. —Google

Dedicated to my husband, Rob.

My one and only.
My guiding compass of true north when I am lost.
My steady ground when I am undone.
My companion, confidant, and the one who always covers my six.

This calling will not fit into a tidy 9-to-5 frame.
There are no parades for MHPs or commendations for the late-night calls, and certainly no applause for the moments I slip away from family to carry the burdens of another.
My work is hidden, heavy, and often lonely.

Yet you are the one who sees me.
You hold the weight I cannot name.
You celebrate the victories—quietly, faithfully, and without needing precious details.
And you give me the good medicine of laughter, reviving me back to life.

This work stands because you hold me up.
Your patience, your strength, and your tenacious cheering are the footing beneath this work.
Though it bears my name, it is written because you are my safe harbor.

And when we feel safe, anything is possible!

Yours always,

Lea

CONTENTS

Welcome Message

from Dr. Lea

MY FIRST MESSAGE to you—as a firefighter and a peer supporter—is this: **Thank You.**

Thank you for your service. Thank you for stepping up, leaning in, and moving your agency forward. Your willingness to dial in when things get complicated—that matters.

Peer support is not just a program—it's the future of mental health in the fire service. And you are part of that powerful and necessary movement.

You are a force. Change will come through you.

This is a responsibility, not a title. Your role is not about having all the answers—it's about being steady when someone else feels shaky. It's about listening without judgment, speaking with skill, and referring with credibility. Others will look to you—not just in crisis, but in the quiet moments that come before it. That trust is earned, and it's serious.

Take it seriously.

But also remember this: **You are not doing this alone.** This playbook is here to equip you, and your team is here to support you. There will be moments that stretch you. You will question yourself sometimes.

That's normal. This work is not easy—but it's real. And it matters.

You have already done something most won't: you said yes to being someone others can count on.

While every peer supporter begins this playbook at Chapter One, no one starts from the same place. Your life experience, your worldview, and the road that brought you here are uniquely yours. And—you are exactly where you need to be.

Stay steady. Stay teachable. Stay in it.

Covering your six,

Lea

Peer Support Role at a Glance

What Peer Support *Is*

- A trusted, trained **crew member who listens and supports**

- A **bridge** to professional help—not a replacement for it

- A **first point of contact** for mental wellness concerns

- A way to **normalize help-seeking** within fire service culture

- A role focused on **listening, guiding, and referring**—not fixing

What Peer Support *Is Not*

- Not a therapist, counselor, or crisis negotiator

- Not a place to **process trauma** or treat mental illness

- Not responsible for **diagnosing** or making treatment decisions

- Not a keeper of **secrets that endanger safety**

- Not a long-term solution or emotional dumping ground

What You *Can* Do

- Be present, listen, and validate without judgment

- Spot warning signs and check in early

- Share vetted resources and encourage action

- Follow up after difficult calls or personal struggles

- Maintain confidentiality—**within safety limits**

- Know when to **bring in backup** and how to do it

Where Your Role Ends

- If there is **suicidal risk, threats, or extreme distress** → bring in backup

- If someone needs to **process trauma** → refer to a clinician

- If you feel you're **in over your head** → consult your team lead or mental health professional (MHP)

- If your own well-being is taking a hit → pull back and get support

Bottom Line

Peer support means having someone's back—**without carrying their full load**. You're the first stop, not the final destination. Your strength is in showing up, listening well, and knowing when to bring in reinforcements. Stay in your lane, trust your limits, and don't hesitate to call in backup. That's how you stay effective—and stay in this work for the long haul.

PART ONE:

The Mission

"A team is not a group of people who work together.
A team is a group of people who trust each other."

— Simon Sinek, *Together Is Better*

---

(1)

THE MISSION

PEER SUPPORT IS NOT about fixing people. It is about standing beside them—eye to eye, shoulder to shoulder—through the hard stuff. As a member of a peer support team, you are not therapists. You are trusted crew members who help bridge the gap between pain and possibility, and the role you play is one of the most effective, immediate, and culturally grounded responses we have to protecting firefighter mental health.

P.R.E.P.

As a peer supporter, you are not just showing up in moments of crisis—you're preparing your crew, your agency, and yourself to handle what comes before, during, and after. The acronym **P.R.E.P.** captures the heart of this role: *Prevention, Response, Engagement, and Pathways.* Each attribute reflects how you bring presence, protection, and leadership to your team's mental wellness. Let's break down what each element means for you in the field.

P – Prevention

Prevention is your quiet superpower. When you invest in building strong, trusting relationships with your crew—checking in regularly, being present without an agenda, creating safe space for honesty—you are already doing the work. Peer supporters are a *protective factor* against burnout, isolation, and suicide because connection is the foundation of overall wellness.

What does prevention look like in action?

- Being consistent: showing up, not just when things go wrong, but every day.

- Asking, "How are you, really?" and waiting for the real answer.

- Creating a culture where vulnerability isn't punished, but respected.

You are not waiting for the wheels to come off—you are helping to keep the rig rolling.

R – Response

When something goes sideways—on the job or at home—peer supporters are often the **first line of support**. That does not mean fixing everything. It means being present, grounded, and calm when someone needs you most.

Whether you are debriefing a tough call, sitting with someone in grief, or reaching out after a noticeable shift in behavior, your presence sends a clear message: *You are not alone in this.*

Response requires:

- Listening without judgment

- Offering confidentiality (within safety limits)

- Knowing when the situation needs to be handed off to professionals

You are not the solution—but you are the one who shows up when it matters most.

E – Engagement

Engagement is what keeps this role alive between the emergencies. It is the regular pulse check—the informal hallway conversations, text check-ins, quick coffee debriefs, and moments of real talk around the dining table. Staying engaged helps you read the room, build rapport, and keep peer support visible and accessible.

It also normalizes mental health conversations. The more you talk about stress, therapy, family strain, and resilience, the more your crewmates will start to see these topics as part of the job—not something to hide or be ashamed of.

Engagement is where trust is built so that *when* a crisis hits, the door is already open.

P – Pathways

Your role is not to be the therapist—it is to **know how to guide someone to a higher level of support**. Peer supporters are connectors. When you recognize that someone needs help beyond what you can offer, you are the bridge to their care.

Pathways include:

- Knowing your department's vetted mental health providers

- Staying updated on local and national crisis resources

- Helping a peer make a call, set up a session, or get time off for care

- Following up to say, "I'm still here. How's it going?"

The goal is not just to talk—it's to move. To help your crews take the next healthy step toward healing.

Peer support teams have a proven track record. They play a **critical and proven role** in protecting the mental health and safety of first responders. Far more than a feel-good initiative, peer support is increasingly recognized as an effective, evidence-based intervention that improves occupational safety, health, and well-being.[1]

Research shows that when a peer supporter steps in—whether it's to check in after a tough call or to walk alongside someone in crisis—they help **break down stigma, increase trust**, and **promote treatment-seeking** behaviors in a population often reluctant to reach out.[2]

Interventions offered by peer supporters have been shown to **boost self-confidence**, encourage **open conversations** about mental health, and more readily **assess serious risks** such as suicidal ideation or harm to others.[3] Additionally, peer support programs not only help crewmates but also positively influence the organization's culture.

What's more, the effectiveness of peer support rises even higher in environments where trust and team cohesion already exist—making it clear that the culture of the crew directly impacts the success of support efforts.[1]

P.R.E.P. is more than a framework—it's your guide to being a solid, effective, and sustainable peer supporter. When you live out **Prevention, Response, Engagement, and Pathways**, you are not just reacting to crises. You are shifting the culture. You're making it normal to struggle and brave to speak up.

And most importantly? You are helping save lives in ways you may never fully see—but the ripple will impact your crew, your agency, and your community.

In short, peer support is not just helpful—it's essential. It has the potential to save careers, relationships, and lives.

Me: Why Am I Doing This?

Take **20–30 minutes** for some self-reflection. Before you can support others, you need to know what is driving you to take on this role. Peer support is not a checkbox—it's a commitment to show up for your crew in their toughest moments. Use the prompts below to guide your reflection. Be honest. Be real. This is not about getting the "right" answers—it's about getting to the *truth*.

- **What first motivated me to become a peer supporter?**
  (Was it a personal experience? Did someone show up—or not—for me when I needed it most?)

7

- **What do I believe about helping others through hard times?** (Do I see it as a responsibility, a calling, a way to give back?)

- What personal values drive me in this serving role?
  (e.g., Compassion? Loyalty? Justice? Integrity?)

- **What am I hoping to protect by being a peer supporter?**
  (My crew's mental health? Our bond? Staying fit for the job?)

Journal your thoughts on the next page.

✎ Journal your thoughts here:

_____

_____

_____

_____

_____

_____

_____

_____

_____

_____

_____

_____

_____

_____

_____

_____

_____

_____

You: Share Your Why

Sharing your self-reflection out loud builds connection, strengthens trust, and helps clarify your own motivations. In this **20–30 minute** exercise, you and a partner will take turns listening and reflecting without judgment or interruption.

Instructions:

1. **Pair up** with another peer supporter.

2. **Partner A** will share their self-reflection. Speak openly about why you chose this role, what drives you, and what challenges you anticipate.

3. **Partner B** listens. No fixing. No interrupting. Just hear them out. After Partner A finishes, Partner B may respond with:

    - "What I heard you say was …" (brief summary)

    - "What stood out to me was …" (a specific point or feeling)

    - "I see strength in you because …"

4. **Switch roles** and repeat.

Time Guide:

- 10 minutes per person to share

- 5 minutes per person for response

Note for both partners: Stay present. This is not about comparing stories— it's about witnessing each other's truth. Be sure to get permission before sharing in the roundtable discussion that follows this exercise.

Us: Remembering Your Why

Let's take **20–30 minutes** for a roundtable discussion with the whole group. The purpose here is to reflect as a team on what motivates each member to serve as a peer supporter, deepen shared purpose, and reinforce personal commitment to the role.

Facilitator Instructions:

1. **Welcome the group back**—Acknowledge the vulnerability and honesty that came through in the partner practice.

   "Thanks for showing up with honesty during the partner practice. Sharing our 'why' puts heart behind this work—and it reminds us that we're not in it alone."

2. **Set the tone**

   - Emphasize psychological safety: there is no pressure to share anything personal.

   - Invite participants to listen with **curiosity**, not judgment.

3. **Ask the group these questions** one at a time. Allow a few participants to respond aloud to each. Use a whiteboard (if available) to capture common themes.

   - *"What came up for you during the partner practice?"*
     (Reword if needed: *"What did this bring up for you?"*)
     → Optional prompt: *"Did anything surprise you about your own why, or your partner's?"*

   - *"How does knowing your Why shape the way you show up in this role?"*
     → Follow-up: *"Does it give you clarity? Energy? A sense of responsibility?"*

11

- *"What risks do we take when we forget our 'why,' or stop checking in with it?"*
  → Encourage discussion around burnout, detachment, or losing purpose.

- *"What's one thing you want to hold onto from today's reflection?"*
  → This could be a word, a phrase, a specific motivation, or even a recommitment.

4. **Wrap-Up Activity—My Action Plan.**

5. ✎ Ask each person to take 2–3 quiet minutes to write down their "why" in one sentence or short paragraph.

   → *"Write it like you are leaving a note to your future self—the version of you that might be tired, discouraged, or second-guessing why you took this on. Make it something you can come back to."*

Option: Provide small cards or sticky notes for participants to take with them or post in a common peer support space.

Closing Words (Facilitator):

Our "why" will not stay the same forever—but checking in with it keeps us grounded. When we lead from purpose, not pressure, we stay more present—for our crew and for ourselves.

(2)

THE LIMITS

THE STRENGTH OF a peer supporter lies not just in their empathy but in their **clarity about boundaries**. While peer support can be deeply personal and powerful, it is not therapy—and knowing where the line is protects both you and the crew member seeking help.

A key boundary for peer supporters is **knowing when to refer**—and having the courage to do it. You are often the first line of defense, but you are not the final stop. When a conversation keeps circling the same pain without forward movement, it's a signal that the issue may be beyond the scope of peer support.

Likewise, if a crewmate begins expressing signs of depression, PTSD, substance misuse, or suicidal thoughts,[4,5] it is not only appropriate, but also it is necessary to involve a mental health professional. These are not situations to "tough out" or to handle solo.

Boundaries do not create distance—they create safety. And in peer support, safety is everything.

Red Flags

Behavioral Red Flags

- **Major shift in personality or behavior** (suddenly withdrawn, irritable, reckless, or numb)

- Noticeable decline in hygiene, grooming, or sleep

- **Increased substance use** or drinking on or off shift

- Talking about feeling hopeless or "done"

- Withdrawing from family, friends, or crew

- Sudden anger outbursts or difficulty controlling emotions

Mental Health Red Flags

- Signs of depression, PTSD, or anxiety that are persistent or worsening

- Ruminating on a call or personal loss with no progress despite support

- **Talking about death** (even passively: "I wouldn't care if I didn't wake up.")

- Flashbacks, nightmares, or emotional numbing

- Difficulty functioning on the job or at home

Communication Red Flags

- Repeating the same story or pain without movement or reflection

- Statements like:
    - o "Nothing's going to help."
    - o "I can't keep doing this."
    - o "You wouldn't understand."
    - o "Don't tell anyone, but …"

These are often signals that your crewmate is stuck—and needs more than peer-level support.

Crisis Red Flags

- Mention of self-harm or suicidal thoughts

- Expressions of wanting to hurt someone else

- Access to means and a specific plan for self-harm

- Domestic violence concerns (as victim or perpetrator)

Peer Supporter Red Flags (For You)

- You feel emotionally drained after each conversation

- You are starting to lose sleep or carry *their* stress home

- You feel stuck, unsure, or in over your head

- You feel like you are the only one keeping them afloat

If any of these apply, it is time to call in backup—for them *and* for you.

If you are asking yourself, "Is this more than I can handle?"—it probably is. And that is not failure. It's leadership. You are not expected to do it all. You *are* expected to know when to hand it off.[2]

Referring for backup isn't failure—**it's a lifeline**. It says, "I care enough to get you the help you deserve." Strong peer supporters know their limits and trust that handing off is part of healing. If you are feeling emotionally drained or overwhelmed, that's a red flag too. Emptying your own well does not help anyone. Referring out protects both of you and keeps support ethical, sustainable, and effective.

Another key boundary essential for peer supporters is understanding the difference between **privacy, confidentiality, and privilege**, especially when navigating sensitive conversations. Here is a clear breakdown tailored for your role:

Privacy refers to a person's right to control their personal information and decide who knows what about them.[6] In peer support, this means respecting someone's choice to open up—or not. You don't push, probe, or share their

---

[2] For tips on vetting a therapist, see the Appendix for a downloadable PDF of Chapter 22 from *Cover My Six: A Comprehensive Guide to Firefighter Care.*

story unless they give clear permission. Simply put: *If it's not yours to tell, don't tell it.*

Confidentiality means keeping what someone shares with you *within the bounds of trust*, unless there is a safety concern.[7] It is the backbone of peer support, creating space for honest conversation. But it has **limits**: if someone shares intent to harm themselves or others, or reveals abuse or serious misconduct, you have a **duty to report**. Peer supporters must be clear from the start: "What you say here stays here—unless you're in danger or someone else is." That kind of up-front honesty builds trust and protects everyone.

Privilege is a legal protection—and peer supporters generally do not have it. While some states, like Washington, North Carolina, and Mississippi, grant limited statutory privilege to designated peer supporters, most do not.[8,9,10] Without a specific law, peer conversations are not legally protected and can be subject to disclosure in court. Confidentiality may be encouraged by policy or ethics, but only privileged communication is legally shielded. States clearly distinguish between the two: *confidential* means private by agreement; *privileged* means protected by law.

If a situation escalates to legal or departmental action, you may be required to share what was discussed. That is why it is crucial to stay within your scope: support, refer, document if required by policy—but do not diagnose or make promises of legal protection.

Clarity in these boundaries does not weaken trust; it *protects* it—by setting honest expectations and keeping your integrity intact. Peer supporters gain trust not by having all the answers, but by being consistently present, real, and respectful of boundaries.

It is tempting to want to reassure someone by saying, "It's going to be okay," or "This will get better soon," but those statements can feel hollow if reality does not match. Instead, be honest: "I don't have all the answers, but I'm here with you, and we'll figure out the next step together." That kind of steady, grounded presence builds a deeper, more lasting trust than any quick fix ever could.

Me: Boundaries in Action

Take **20–30 minutes** to reflect honestly on your comfort level with setting and holding boundaries as a peer supporter. Boundaries protect both you and your peers—but they can be hard to navigate in the moment.

- How comfortable am I with **recognizing when something is beyond my scope** and needs referral to a professional?

- Have I ever hesitated to refer someone because I didn't want to let them down—or feared they would shut down?

- How clear am I when I explain the **limits of confidentiality**? Do I give people a false sense of protection, or am I direct and transparent?

- What is one situation where I **struggled with a boundary**? What would I do differently now?

- How do I handle it when a peer keeps coming back with the same pain but is not moving forward?

Write down your thoughts. There is no "right" answer—just an honest one. Boundaries are not barriers—they are the structure that allows this work to stay safe, sustainable, and strong.

✎ Journal your thoughts here:

You: Practicing Boundaries

This **20-30 minute** exercise will help you and your partner build skills and confidence in setting boundaries around **referral** and **confidentiality**.

Instructions:

1. **Partner up** with other peer supporter—Partner A plays a peer supporter and Partner B plays a crewmember in need of support (then you switch).

2. **Read the scenario — Stuck in the Story.** Your crewmate keeps looping through details of a traumatic call weeks ago. They have come to you three times but have not taken any steps forward.

   - Practice the Conversation – Focus on explaining the limits of confidentiality clearly and calmly.

   - Emphasize listening with empathy while staying grounded in your role.

   - Pay careful attention to deciding whether referral is appropriate—and how to bring it up.

3. **Now switch roles.**

4. **Read the scenario — Confidentiality Testing.** Your crewmate says, "You can't tell anyone, but I've been thinking a lot about how it might be better if I just didn't wake up."

   - Practice the Conversation – Focus on explaining the limits of confidentiality clearly and calmly.

- Emphasize listening with empathy while staying grounded in your role.

- Pay careful attention to deciding whether referral is appropriate—and how to bring it up.

5. **Debrief together**—Reflect on:

   - What felt natural or difficult?

   - Did you overstep or hesitate anywhere?

   - How did it feel to protect both connection and boundaries?

Us: What Hit Home?

Let's take **30 minutes** to debrief as a group. Boundaries are not just about rules—they bring up real tension between wanting to help and knowing when to step back. This roundtable discussion will help your team normalize the emotional and ethical complexity of knowing when to help, when to refer, and how to honor confidentiality.

Facilitator Instructions:

1. **Welcome the Group Back**
   Acknowledge that setting boundaries isn't just about following protocol—it often brings up emotional tension and internal conflict. Say something like:

   "Let's take some time to process what came up. Boundaries are not about cold rules—they're about protecting relationships and staying

grounded in our role. The more we talk about them, the more skilled and confident we become."

2. Set the Ground Rules

   • Normalize discomfort: *"It's okay if some of that felt awkward or heavy."*

   • Encourage honest reflections—no judgment, just shared learning.

3. Ask one question at a time and give space for responses. You can jot down key words or common themes on a board or flip chart, if helpful.

   • *"What parts of the conversation felt easy? What felt hard?"*
     → Optional prompt: *"Was it easier to listen or to draw a line?"*

   • *"How did it feel to clearly state the limits of confidentiality?"*
     → *"Did it come out naturally, or did it feel like a script?"*

   • *"Did anyone notice yourself wanting to 'fix it' instead of refer?"*
     → *"What internal pressure or impulse came up?"*

   • *"What were your internal signals that it was time to hand off or bring in more support?"*
     → Encourage examples of gut feelings, emotional fatigue, or moments of uncertainty.

   • *"How can we support each other when a boundary call feels heavy?"*
     → Invite the group to share language, habits, or team practices that help.

4. Wrap-Up Activity—My Action Plan.
   ✎ Ask each participant to write down (privately, in their workbook):

- One boundary I will practice communicating more clearly is:

- When I feel unsure, I will reach out to:

- A phrase I can use when I need to refer or step back is:

Closing Words (Facilitator):

(Use words most comfortable for you).

"Boundaries are not walls—they're clarity. They protect both the peer and the supporter. Every time we practice them, we are building trust and sustainability into this role. It's okay to not always get it perfect. What matters is that we keep learning, together."

PART TWO:

Core Competencies

"A journey of a thousand miles
begins with a single step."

— Laozi, *Tao Te Ching* (Chapter 64)

---

(3)

TACTICAL LISTENING

THE GOAL OF Tactical Listening is to help the other person feel heard and understood—from their lens. These supportive conversations are not about fixing, advising, or inserting your opinion. The win is not walking away with a solution. The win is walking away with the other person feeling like:

- "They see me, and they really hear me."

- "They understand where I am coming from."

- "I don't have to justify or explain every word—I can just be real."

That is tactical listening. And the mission is connection. This kind of listening is intentional, disciplined, and mission focused.

The DOs of Tactical Listening

DO clear your agenda. Your only goal is to listen while being fully present. Bring your whole self to the conversation. Set aside any urge to educate, correct, or counterpoint.

DO use body language that communicates emotional safety. Use open posture. Give steady eye contact without staring. Keep a calm tone. Nod to show you are tracking with what they are saying. These are the unspoken cues that say, *I'm here. I'm with you. I'm listening.*

DO listen to understand, not to respond. If you are already thinking about what you will say next, you are not truly listening. Stay in their story and don't get stuck in your response.

DO ask curious and open-ended questions. Questions that start with *What* (rather than *Why*) offer space to explore the other person's experience without judgment or pressure of needing a "right" response.

Invite curiosity by saying phrases like "tell me more" or "I wonder …," which encourages openness and signals acceptance of the other person's experience. Curious and open-ended questions are like a preventive salve—softening the space between you, reducing the risk of defensiveness before it flares, and creating a sense of safety that allows people to go deeper. Some examples are:

- "What was that like for you?"

- "Tell me more about that."

- "I wonder what that feeling is all about."

DO validate their experience. Validation is **not** agreement! It is acknowledging the other person's lived and very real experience. It is not *in*validating your own, should your experience be wildly different. It is recognizing the humanity and perspective of another. Even if (and perhaps, especially *when*) you do not agree with their interpretation, you can validate their emotions and the impact they have experienced. Some powerfully validating responses are:

- "That sounds like it really hit hard."

- "I can hear/see how much that's been weighing on you."

- "It makes perfect sense that you'd feel this way."

DO reflect back what you hear, using their words. Words convey meaning, and using *their* words when paraphrasing back what you hear shows that you are tracking their experience, from their lens. **This is one of the most helpful tools in your peer support toolbox** and is so simple that it is often overlooked. A person is more likely to feel truly heard and deeply understood when you use the language that packs the most meaning *for them.* Then follow up with a check-in to make sure you are on track. This builds trust, fosters a sense of connection, and gives the other person an opportunity to expand or clarify their experience.

- "So what I'm hearing is you felt blindsided by that?"

- "Am I getting it?"

- "Help me out here; it sounds like you felt stuck between a rock and a hard spot. Is that right?"

DO hold space for silence. Silence is not an empty void—it's a space for process. Let them consider, sort their emotions out, and take a moment to breathe. Silence can be an effective tool that helps their brain settle and de-escalate.

The DON'Ts of Tactical Listening

DON'T hijack the conversation. Turning the conversation to yourself, even with a well-intentioned story that relates, erodes the very trust and understanding that you are trying to build. Avoid phrases like *"This reminds me of when I—."* If you hear yourself redirecting the conversation toward your own experience, simply stop. This is not your moment to feel heard and understood. Let them have the floor.

DON'T play devil's advocate. This is not the time to offer a different perspective or to try to balance out their thinking by saying, *"Well, have you thought about it this way?"* Even if their view is incomplete or has blind spots—leave it. Your mission right now is for them to feel heard and understood *from their lens.*

DON'T rush to fix or offer solutions. Advice offered too early can feel dismissive. Just wait. Most people, especially when feeling anxious, angry, or sad, need to feel heard *before* they are ready to think clearly.

DON'T downplay, minimize, or compare their feelings. Trying to cheer someone up can accidently invalidate what they are feeling, causing them to minimize or dismiss their own hurt or suffering. Avoid phrases like:

- "That's just a normal Monday."

- "You'll be fine. It'll all work out."

- "It could be worse. Other people have it worse."

DON'T interrupt or correct details. Let go of accuracy or balance in the moment. Whether they are missing a detail or exaggerating does not matter in this moment. Their *experience* is what matters most.

DON'T multitask. Checking your phone or scanning the room says: *You're not my priority.* Be fully present. That's where the magic happens.

Tactical Listening is not passive. It's not just sitting there nodding—it's actively choosing to climb into their experience and see the world from their vantage point. You do not have to agree. You do not have to endorse every word. You just have to *understand.*

When someone truly feels heard, it softens their defenses and opens the door to real connection. That's when trust is built, and healing begins. Tactical Listening will help get you there.

Me: Self-Reflection on Tactical Listening

Before we can be fully present for someone else, we have to get honest with ourselves. Tactical Listening starts with self-awareness. Be honest. Be curious—not critical. This is not about perfection. It's about growth.

1. When someone shares something hard with me, what is my first instinct?

☐ Jump into problem-solving?

☐ Try to help them see a silver lining?

☐ Share a story of my own?

☐ Pause and listen without needing to respond?

2. How comfortable am I with silence in a conversation?

☐ I feel the need to fill it right away.

☐ I can tolerate it for a bit, but it feels awkward.

☐ I trust silence as part of the process.

3. What's hardest for me about Tactical Listening?

☐ Staying present

☐ Letting go of my opinion

☐ Not interrupting

☐ Trusting that listening *is* doing something

4. What helps me listen better?

☐ Taking a breath before I speak

☐ Reminding myself: "This is not about me"

☐ Making eye contact and staying grounded

☐ Mentally clearing my own stress before the conversation

☐ Practicing with trusted peers

Tactical Listening is not about being a perfect responder, it's about being a present one. What is one way you can lean in a little more this week—listening with curiosity, calm, and connection? Take 20-30 minutes to reflect and journal on the next page.

✎ Journal your thoughts here:

You: Tactical Listening in Action

This is not about solving, fixing, or agreeing. Your mission is to help the other person feel *heard* and *understood*—from their lens. In this **20–30-minute** exercise, you will practice listening with curiosity, validation, reflection, and presence.

Instructions:
Partner up. Decide who will be the **Speaker** and who will be the **Listener** first. You'll switch roles halfway through.

Speaker's Role: Share something real. Not your deepest secret, but something meaningful—a frustration, a recent stressor, or something that's been weighing on you. Simply speak from your experience.

Peer Supporter's Role: Your goal is connection—not correction. Practice the following:

- **Start with curiosity.** Use "I wonder …" and "Tell me more…" to invite them deeper into their story.

- **Validate what you hear.** Use phrases like:
  "That makes sense."
  "That sounds like it really hit hard."
  "I can hear how much that's been weighing on you."

- **Reflect back their words.** Use their exact or close-to-exact wording. Try:
  "So what I'm hearing is …"
  "It sounds like …"

- **Hold space with silence.** Do not rush to fill the quiet. Let the silence do some of the heavy lifting.

Practice your role for 10-15 minutes, then switch roles.

Us: Roundtable Discussion

After the partner exercise, bring the group back together for a **20–30-minute** roundtable debrief. This is where the deeper learning happens—not just from your own experience, but by hearing the perspectives of others around you.

Facilitator Tip: Create a space of safety and respect. Emphasize that this is not a performance—this is about sharpening the skill of presence, one rep at a time.

Facilitator Instructions: Go around the circle and invite each person to respond to one or more of the questions below.

Roundtable Prompts:

1. *"What did you notice when you really set aside your own perspective and just listened?"*

2. *"Was it easier or harder than you expected?"*

3. *What was it like to use "I wonder ... " or "Tell me more ... "? "Did it change the direction or depth of the conversation?"*

4. *"What did you learn about the power of silence?" "Was it awkward? Useful? Did it create space for something unexpected?"*

5. *"As the speaker, what helped you feel safe or heard?" "Was there something your partner did that really made a difference?"*

6. *"What surprised you most during the exercise?" "Something about yourself, your partner, or the process?"*

7. *"What's one thing you want to carry forward into real conversations— on or off shift?"*

Wrap-Up Thought:

"Listening with this level of presence is a discipline. It builds trust, disarms defensiveness, and opens doors for connection that advice never could. The goal is not perfect technique—it's authentic presence."

(4)

RESILIENT
RESPONDING

RESILIENCE IS NOT just a buzzword. In the science of human relationships, it has a name: **secure attachment**. When people have dependable, supportive, emotionally attuned relationships—what researchers call *secure attachment bonds*—they are better equipped to handle adversity. The evidence is clear: secure attachment reduces the long-term impact of trauma, promotes psychological flexibility (holding conflicting ideas at the same time), increases self-efficacy (belief in yourself), lowers anxiety and depression, and even enhances creativity and problem-solving capacity.

Whether in childhood, adulthood, romantic partnerships, or peer support relationships, secure connection is the single most protective factor for mental health across the life span. As Bowlby (1982) wrote, "Attachment behavior is held to characterize human beings from the cradle to the grave."[11]

This is especially relevant in the fire service, where **avoidant and anxious attachment styles are disproportionately common.**[12] These patterns often develop as a response to chronic stress, high-performance expectations, and a culture that rewards emotional suppression over vulnerability. Left unaddressed, these styles can erode connection, increase emotional isolation, and reduce resilience over time. But here's the good news: **secure attachment can be cultivated**, even in high-stress professions, and especially in the job of fire service.

In this culture, you do not always control what you face—but you *can* shape how you face it, together. Peer supporters are in a unique position to foster secure bonds within crews. When you offer connection, accessibility, responsiveness, and engagement—what we call a C.A.R.E. Conversation— you are doing so much more than listening. You are helping build the psychological scaffolding that makes recovery, reflections, and resilience possible.

Resilience is the outcome. C.A.R.E. Conversations are the process.

C.A.R.E. Conversations

C — Connection

The emotional bond that says: "You matter here. You are not alone."

Connection is the cornerstone of a secure attachment. According to the founding researchers on attachment, infants and children who felt emotionally connected to a caregiver had better stress regulation and exploration behaviors.[13] That same principle applies to adults. When people feel emotionally tethered, they can face stress more functionally.[14]

In peer support, connection starts with presence—being attuned and nonjudgmental and showing genuine interest. Even brief moments of authentic connection can buffer against burnout, increase morale, and help someone feel seen.

A — Accessibility

"When I reach for you, will you be there?"

The question of accessibility is central to secure attachment. The father of attachment, John Bowlby (1969 & 1982), emphasized that the predictability and availability of an attachment figure was what made them "secure."[15,16] In peer relationships, this means being reachable—not just physically, but emotionally as well. It is being someone your crew can count on, not only during a crisis, but in the in-between moments too.

Making yourself accessible does not mean having all the answers. It does mean being willing to show up—calm, grounded, and open.

R — Responsiveness

"When I need you most, will you join me?"

Responsiveness is the active part of emotional availability. Researchers have found that when someone responds to distress with care and sensitivity, it helps regulate emotional distress, builds trust, and strengthens resilience.[17]

In peer support, this means not fixing or minimizing, but responding with validation, empathy, and curiosity. It is showing that you are emotionally moved by what they are sharing, not just checking a box. It's letting someone know: *What you are going through matters, and I am here with you in it.*

39

E — Engagement

"Are you emotionally present and here with me, right now?"

Engagement is what turns a conversation into connection. Dr. Sue Johnson, founder of Emotionally Focused Therapy (2008), identified Engagement—being present and involved—as one of the three pillars of secure adult attachment, alongside Accessibility and Responsiveness.[18] Engagement is not about offering solutions—it's about being emotionally present. It is sustained eye contact, leaning in, listening between the lines. It's staying with the hard emotions instead of retreating or distracting with humor.

In peer support, engagement is how we hold space for another person. It tells someone: *You are worth my full attention, right here, right now.*

When you lead with C.A.R.E.—when you offer **Connection, Accessibility, Responsiveness, and Engagement**—you are doing more than being supportive. You are building **resilience** at the attachment level. You are helping someone answer the core question: *Am I safe, seen, and supported here?*

And when the answer is yes, people recover faster. They make meaning. They move forward.

Me: How Do I Show Up?

Secure attachment does not just happen—it's built through repeated moments of connection, accessibility, responsiveness, and engagement. As a peer supporter, you are both a witness and a builder of secure attachment. Take a quiet **20–30 minutes** to reflect on the following questions. Be honest. Be curious. No judgment—just observation.

C – Connection

✎. Who in my circle do I feel most emotionally connected to?

_____

_____

_____

✎. When was the last time I let someone know they mattered—outside of a crisis?

_____

_____

_____

A – Accessibility

✎. When people reach for me, how do I show that I am available?

_____

_____

_____

✎. Are there ways I unintentionally signal I'm _too busy, disengaged, or emotionally shut down_?

_____

_____

_____

R – Responsiveness

✎. How do I usually respond when someone shares something hard or emotional?

_____

_____

_____

✎. Do I tend to problem-solve, change the subject, or hold space?

_____

_____

_____

E – Engagement

✎. When I'm in conversation, am I fully present—or mentally checking out?

_____

_____

_____

✎. What helps me stay engaged with someone else's pain, especially when I cannot fix it?

_____

_____

_____

You: C.A.R.E. Conversations in Action

This **20–30-minute** partner practice will help you build confidence and skill in offering *Connection, Accessibility, Responsiveness, and Engagement* during real-time peer support conversations.

Instructions: Partner up. Decide who will be the **Speaker** and who will be the **Listener** first. Each partner will have 10–15 minutes to practice their role, then you'll switch roles.

Speaker: Brings a real (non-crisis) experience that stirred stress, frustration, or vulnerability—at work or at home. Here are some prompts to get you started:

- A time I felt overwhelmed at work was …

- One of the harder parts of this job for me is …

- Something I've been carrying lately …

Peer Supporter: Practices the C.A.R.E. model to offer supportive presence, not solutions. Put the prompts into phrases that work best for you.

Connection—Start by *noticing* and *naming* what's coming up.

- "Thanks for trusting me with that."

- "That sounds like a heavy moment."

Accessibility—Show up emotionally and stay available.

- Body language: eye contact, open posture, minimal distractions

- "I'm here with you. Keep going if you're willing."

Responsiveness—Validate, reflect, and invite.

- "I hear that you felt _____."

- "That makes sense to me."

- "Tell me more about that."

Engagement—Stay attuned. Let there be silence. Lean in with empathy.

- "What was the hardest part of that for you?"

- "How are you holding up with it now?"

Us: Group Table Talk

After practicing in pairs, gather as a full peer support team to reflect together. This is not a performance—this is about growing your awareness, building your confidence, and strengthening your connection as a team.

Facilitator Instructions:

Open the floor by saying something like: *"Let's take a few minutes to unpack what that experience was like. This is where we grow our insight—not just our skills. You don't need to have the 'right answer.' Just speak from what was real for you."*

Group Discussion Prompts:

Go around the room or open it up popcorn-style. Invite participants to reflect on:

1. Which part of C.A.R.E. came most naturally to you?

- Was it connecting emotionally? Staying present? Asking follow-up questions?

2. What felt awkward, hard, or unfamiliar?

- Did you notice a tendency to jump in with advice or try to fix? Was it hard to sit with silence?

3. How did it feel to be truly heard—and not fixed?

- What was it like to have someone simply be with you instead of do something?

4. Did anything shift in how you usually show up for others?

- Did this exercise change how you think about listening or support?

Wrap with a shared insight or takeaway (in words most comfortable for you): *"Let's each offer one word or phrase that captures what we're walking away with from this experience—whether it's a feeling, a realization, or something you want to take back to your crew."*

Facilitator Tips:

- **Model vulnerability.** Go first if needed—share what *you* found hard or surprising and leave space for others!

- **Honor silence.** Let pauses breathe. That is part of what you are teaching and learning.

- **Remind the group:** *"This is not about being perfect. It's about being present. You don't need fancy words—you need a grounded heart."*

(5)

THE CALL
AFTER THE CALL

SOME CALLS ARE OVER when the rigs return to the bay.

Others are not.

The emotional weight, physiological overload, or images that linger often hit afterward. That's why peer support does not end when you clear the scene. In fact, what happens *after* the call often shapes resilience the most.

Following a tough call, peer support teams should be ready to apply **emergent care**—brief, in-the-moment support that helps stabilize a peer who is not in crisis but isn't okay, either.

Apply emergent care when you notice:

- Emotional shutdown or body numbing

- Withdrawal, silence, or irritability

- Pacing, agitation, or restlessness

- Flat affect, glassy eyes, or frozen posture

- Signs of overwhelm ("I can't shake this one" / "This one got to me")

- Repeating the same details of the call over and over. This is a signal that the brain is trying—but struggling—to process what happened. It's a cue that they may need a C.A.R.E. conversation or somatic grounding to help settle the overload.

These signs can manifest immediately or up to a few weeks following the incident. Some symptoms do not show up right away—so keep your eye on your crewmates. Staying aware of your crewmates' behavior over time is part of your role as a peer supporter.

Emergent care bridges the gap between injury and recovery. It's how we turn disconnection into reconnection—the first step toward healing.

How to engage:

- **Find privacy, not pressure.** Step aside casually. "You good?" is not enough. Try something like: "That was a tough one. Want to grab a coffee for a few minutes?"

- **Use Tactical Listening and C.A.R.E. Conversations.** Let them lead. Validate their reality. Reflect what you hear. Do not minimize. Do not fix.

- **Look and listen for signs of nervous system overload.** If their body is still in threat mode (agitated, numb, unable to articulate), move toward grounding.

When the body stays activated, talking alone will not bring relief. We need somatic tools *first*—methods that downshift the nervous system, bringing it back into balance. Here are a few key tools:

The Basics of Somatic Tools

Mind-Body Bridging and Tactical Breathing are a few of the trauma-informed approaches that help shift people from stress-based thinking to present-moment awareness.[19] While *Cover My Six* is not affiliated with nor endorsed by any specific techniques, the following is a simple, field-tested version of those strategies—adapted to help you guide a peer in the heat of the moment.

Step 1: Notice

"What's going on in your body right now? Where do you feel it—chest, stomach, neck?"

Let them name it. No need to fix it. Naming is the first bridge.

Step 2: Map Your Senses

Ask them to name 3 things they see, 2 things they hear, 1 thing they physically feel.

This brings them out of hyperarousal or shutdown and back into the here and now.

Step 3: Shift the Loop

Say something like: "Let's just breathe here for a minute. You're safe now. The call is over."

This reinforces that the body can begin to down-regulate.

Additional Grounding Strategies:

- **Cold water** (wrists, neck) to stimulate the vagus nerve

- **Box breathing** (4-in, 4-hold, 4-out, 4-hold)

- **Foot tapping or pacing** to discharge excess energy

- **Simple movement** (walking, shoulder rolls, deep sighs)

Grounding is the first line of defense against a trauma impact. It helps calm the stress response *before* it cements into trauma. It also helps downregulate or downshift the brain so that it can take in new information. When the body is on high alert and activated, the nervous system must settle before problem-solving or clear reasoning are possible. That is why grounding is a critical first step in building resilience against the impact of trauma

Sometimes a difficult call affects **the whole crew**. In these moments, **group-based care** can be a lifeline.

CISD vs. CISM: Know the Difference

- *Critical Incident Stress Debriefing (CISD)* is a formal, structured, one-time group process, typically led by trained professionals.

- *Critical Incident Stress Management (CISM)* is broader—includes pre-incident education, defusing, individual check-ins, and follow-up support.

When to use group care:

- After high-impact calls

- When multiple members express distress or continue repeating the same details of the story ("I just don't understand")

- When silence and avoidance start spreading through the team (i.e., everyone is *handling it* on their own—some go work out, some eat ice cream, others go to their bunks)

Tips for facilitating or advocating for group care:

- Debriefing in some form can and should be led by a peer support team member who was <u>not</u> affiliated with the critical incident call.

- Let people name what they're carrying, **without forced sharing**.

- Normalize a post-incident group roundtable as a part of your SOP. This is just a discussion. A simple way to shake off what they witnessed.

- Create **psychological safety**: voluntary attendance, no rank-based judgment, confidentiality.

- Validate emotional reactions as *normal responses to exceptional events.*

- Leading post-incident care requires specialized training and should always involve two facilitators: one to guide the discussion, the other to monitor participants—especially those who remain quiet.

You train relentlessly for the call—but the most overlooked part of the job is what happens afterward. This is where peer support becomes essential.

Whether it's a hallway check-in, a lap around the station, a group debrief, or a quiet moment to ground with a partner—every small act after the call can interrupt potential trauma and plant the seeds of recovery.

Me: The Moments That Linger

Some calls fade quickly. Others remain. Oftentimes it is not even the worst call—it's the one that caught you off guard or hit too close to home. This **20–30-minute** reflection helps you pause, check in with yourself, and consider how you have responded *after* the call—both for yourself and for others. Take a few minutes in a quiet place. No need to judge. Just notice.

Reflecting on a Past Call—Think of a call that stuck with you longer than expected.

- What do you remember feeling **right after** it ended?

- How did your **body** react—tight chest, buzzing limbs, total numbness?

- What did you do with those feelings—talk to someone, bury them, distract yourself?

Grounding and Support—What, if anything, helped you feel more grounded afterward?

- Was there someone who said or did something helpful?

- Did you try to "tough it out" alone?

- Looking back, what kind of **support or care** would have helped most in that moment?

Your Role with Others—When someone else is impacted by a call, what is your default response?

- Do you check in? Avoid it? Crack a joke? Wait for them to bring it up?

- What part of emergent care—**Connection, Grounding, Listening, or Partner Inclusion**—feels most natural to you?

- Which one do you want to grow in?

✎. **If you could go back and offer yourself one thing after that tough call, what would it be?** Write a short note to your past self. Make it what you needed to hear then—and what you may need again in the future.

You: Reading Between the Lines

This **20–30-minute** exercise gives you a chance to practice a C.A.R.E. conversation—reaching out to a brother or sister who is showing early signs of stress but brushing it off like it's no big deal. It's about learning how to check in without pushing, and showing up in a way that actually lands.

Partner 1: Firefighter recently involved in a critical incident (e.g., pediatric fatality, suicide, or gruesome call). They're starting to show subtle signs of stress—short temper, trouble sleeping, zoning out, or joking more darkly than usual—but they brush it off with: "It's fine. Just a busy week."

Partner 2: Peer supporter. You've worked with them long enough to know something is off. You are not here to confront—you are here to *connect* and *create space* for what might be going on beneath the surface.

Step 1: Reach Out—Privacy, Not Pressure

Start a low-stakes conversation that offers *presence without pressure.*

Try something like this: *"Hey, we've been on a string of rough calls lately. You up for a quick walk around the bay?"* Or *"You've seemed a little off the last couple days—could be nothing, but I wanted to check in. Mind if we grab coffee outside for a few?"*

Step 2: Use C.A.R.E. + Tactical Listening

Once you're in a private, low-stress environment, shift into a **C.A.R.E. Conversation**.

Connection—Start with authentic concern: *"That last call hit differently. You haven't said much since. What's been sticking with you—if anything?"* Let the silence stretch. No pressure to respond right away.

Accessibility—Be emotionally present: *"I don't need the polished version—just what's real."* Use tone, posture, and pace to stay grounded and available.

Responsiveness—Validate without minimizing: *"That makes sense."* Or *"I've been there too—where it sneaks up later and you don't even realize it's still with you."* If they brush it off, respond with something like *"You say it's nothing, but your body might be telling a different story. Sleep off? Snapping more than usual?"*

Engagement—Stay curious: *"What part of that call keeps flashing back, even a little?"*; *"What's your gut been holding onto?"*; *"What's your body been saying—tight chest, foggy head, restlessness?"*

Step 3: Validate, Reflect, and Hold Space

Use **mirroring and summarizing**: *"So you've been snapping at home and not sleeping, but you're not sure it's from the call—am I getting it here?"* Then pause. Let silence do its work. *"You don't have to name it all. Just know I've got time, and I'm not in a rush to move past it."*

Step 4: Look and Listen for Nervous System Overload

Watch for:

- Shallow breathing or holding breath

- Fidgeting or freezing

- Flat tone or detached speech

- Hypervigilance (startled by noises, scanning the room)

- Emotional flatness or sudden anger

If you see these signs, say something like: *"I wonder if your body's still stuck in that mode—even if your brain says you're fine."* Then transition into grounding.

Step 5: Guide to Grounding (When Needed)

"Let's just hit pause for a sec. You don't need to talk—just follow my lead."

Use any of these:

- **Box Breathing:** In for 4... hold for 4... out for 4... hold for 4.

- **3-2-1:** *"Tell me 3 things you see. 2 things you can hear. 1 thing you feel ..."*

- **Cold water on wrists or neck**

- **Pace the room** slowly together

End with a reassuring phrase that joins you. Something like: *"You're not on that call anymore. You're here. You are not alone."*

57   © 2025 by Dr. Lea Sullivan

Us: Group Reflection

Reflect as a group on how to approach a crewmate who is showing signs of stress after a tough call but downplays or dismisses it. This **20–30-minute** conversation is about *growing your awareness*, not getting it perfect.

Facilitator Instruction:

Open with something like *"That scenario—the one where someone's clearly not okay but says they're fine—is one of the most common peer support moments. Let's talk through what it felt like to step into that space. No judgment, just reflection."*

Discussion Prompts:

Use these questions to guide an open discussion. Let participants speak as they feel ready. Silence is okay. Reflection takes time.

1. What helped open the door?

- What wording, tone, or approach felt most natural to reach out without pushing?

- What was one thing you said (or heard) that shifted the dynamic?

2. What felt hard or awkward?

- Where did you feel yourself hesitate?

- What part made you want to pull back or change the subject?

3. What signs of stress did you notice?

- How did their body language, tone, or pacing suggest nervous system overload?

- What subtle signs told you they were not actually fine?

4. What did grounding do for the moment?

- Did it change the feel of the conversation?

- What's one grounding tool you now feel more confident using?

5. How does this change how you'll show up next time?

- What's one thing you'll carry forward into future calls?

- What do you want to remember next time someone says they're fine—but you know they're not?

Closing the Roundtable—Each supporter shares one word or phrase that captures what they are taking away from this exercise—something they are learning, noticing, or committing to.

(6)

CRISIS RESPONSE

PEER SUPPORTERS ARE HERE to listen—not fix, diagnose, or treat. But sometimes, the conversation shifts. Something said or left unsaid signals your internal tones. This chapter is about what to do when that shift happens—when someone's life, safety, or mental stability may be at risk.

Let's be clear: If someone is at risk of suicide, self-harm, or harming others, it is no longer a peer conversation. It is a **crisis**. The goal is not to decide if it is "serious enough." The goal is to act and to get them to safety.

What to Do in High-Risk Cases

There is nothing wrong with trusting your gut—but that only works if you have trained your gut to respond. Here are some clear signs that require escalation:[20,21]

- Direct or indirect talk of suicide
    - "I don't want to be here anymore."
    - "It would be easier if I just disappeared."
    - "Everyone would be better off without me."
- Mentions of self-harm or history of attempts
- Loss of control, disorientation, or talking in circles
- Expressions of hopelessness, unbearable pain, or being a burden
- Access to lethal means (weapons, medications, etc.)
- Withdrawal from all supports
- Giving away belongings or saying goodbye

If you are seeing or hearing these—**do not ignore or downplay them**. You are not overreacting by taking action. You are protecting a life.

Emergency Protocols

1. **Stay with them.** Your presence matters more than perfect words. Remain calm. Grounded. Tuned in.

2. **Start by expressing your concern and desire to help.** Helpful phrases are:

   "I'm worried because I noticed you [insert things you've noticed]. How can I help you through this?"

   "It seems like you have been up and down lately. I've been there myself. Talking about it really helps."

3. **Ask directly.** Research is clear: asking about suicide does **not** plant the idea and actually brings them **relief.**[22] By naming it out loud, they finally have someone acknowledging how bad they are feeling. It opens a door that might save their life!

   "Are you thinking about suicide?"

   "Have you thought about how you'd do it?"

   "Do you have access to [gun, pills, etc.] right now?"

4. **Remain calm if they say yes.** Just because someone is having thoughts of suicide does not mean they are in immediate danger. Take time to calmly listen and ask open-ended follow-up questions to better assess their risk level.

5. **Be transparent about confidentiality.** Be real with them—this is bigger than the two of you. Let them know you are not going to carry this alone, and they don't have to either. Say something like:

   "You're not in trouble, and you're not too much—this is bigger than both of us. I care about you too much to keep it to myself."

   "I care about you too much not to take this seriously."

   "We both need some backup right now. I've got you."

You are **not** handing them off. You **are** staying with them—just bringing in backup support.

6. **Activate the Red Flag Flowchart** (see below). Know your department's SOP. When in doubt, err on the side of safety.

7. **Contact an officer, clinician, chaplain, or critical incident team member.** If you're unsure whom to call, start with the National Suicide & Crisis Lifeline: **988**. They'll walk you through it. You don't have to do this alone.

Red Flag Flowchart

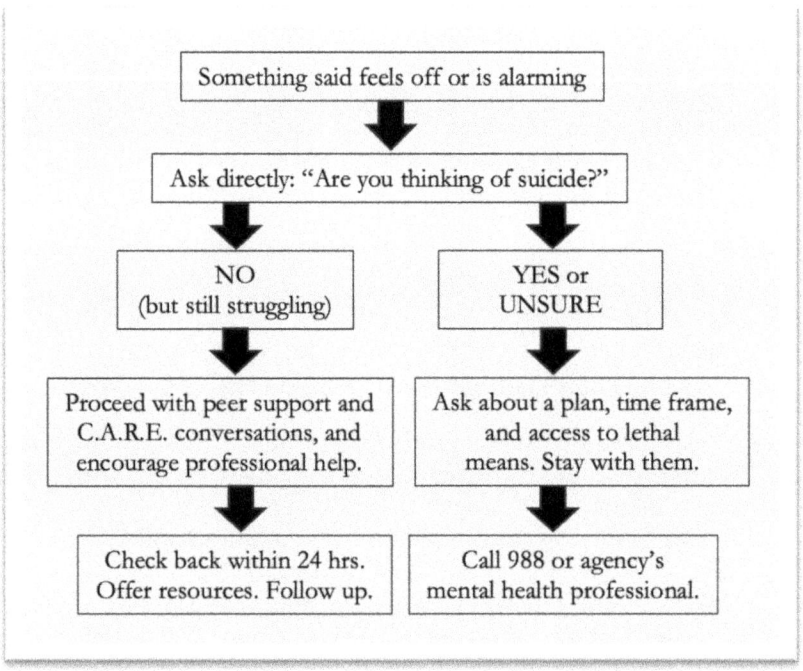

Note: If they say yes, and have a plan, means, and intent → *this is an emergency*. Don't leave them alone. Call for backup. Ride with them if they go to the hospital (or better yet, drive them yourself). **Show up as a human**, not just a responder.

If Weapons Are Involved

If there is access to a firearm and you are concerned for their safety:

- Ask directly: "Do you have access to your gun right now?"

- Involve law enforcement, chaplain, or designated MHP if needed.

- Explore voluntary temporary storage (e.g., with trusted family member).

This is a hard line to walk in first-responder culture. But nothing is worth more than a life.

Self-Care for the Peer Responder

Being present for someone in crisis is emotionally taxing. Afterward:

- **Debrief with a clinician, chaplain, or another peer supporter.**

- **Check in with yourself.** Don't minimize your own stress.

- **Don't disappear.** Support isn't just one moment—it's follow-through. Stay connected with check-ins and C.A.R.E. conversations.

- **Log the event if required.** Protect your integrity and track patterns.

Crisis moments do not follow scripts. But you do not have to panic when they show up. You're not alone—and neither is the person sitting across from you. If you remember nothing else, remember this:

Connection saves lives.

You are a bridge between someone who is suffering and the help they need. And sometimes, all someone needs is to know that they matter and that they are not alone.

To download the free PDF
Personal Crisis Preplan, **see the Appendix.**

Me: When the Stakes Are High

In crisis moments, your calm may be a lifeline for someone else. As firefighters, you apply this reality on scene and during every shift. This chapter walked you through how to respond when someone is at risk of self-harm or suicide. Now it is time to slow down, pause, and check in—with yourself.

Take 20–30 quiet minutes. Breathe. Then answer honestly:

✎ **When someone is in distress and I feel overwhelmed or unsure of what to say, do I tend to lean in—or back away?**

_____

_____

_____

✎. **Have I ever hesitated to ask directly about suicide?** If so, what stopped me—fear, discomfort, not wanting to make it worse?

_____

_____

_____

✎. **What are the differences between my role and the role of a therapist or mental health professional?** Can I recognize that supporting someone does not mean "fixing" them or their situation?

_____

_____

_____

✎. **Have I practiced grounding myself before showing up for someone else?** What helps me stay present under pressure?

_____

_____

_____

✎ **When was the last time I checked in on *my own* stress or burnout levels?** On a scale of 1–10, (1 = my best life; 10 = I'm running on empty), where am I at today?

_____

_____

_____

✎ **Final prompt:** When someone comes to me in crisis, I want to be someone who:

_____

_____

_____

Finish the sentence. No fluff. Just the truth. You cannot control outcomes. But you *can* train your nervous system, sharpen your awareness, and build the courage to act. That is what sets you apart as a prepared peer supporter.

You: Crisis Response Drill

You know the drill. Partner up. Practice this crisis response drill for **20–30 minutes**, switching roles halfway through. Strong emotions may surface. It's okay—you will process those feelings during the group roundtable following this exercise.

Scenario: A firefighter does not quite seem themselves on shift. They are quieter and withdrawn and their dark humor has taken a sharper edge. You have noticed. And today, something they said hits differently.

Partner 2 (Peer supporter):

Initiate the conversation, saying something like: "Hey—can I check in with you real quick? You've been on my mind. I've noticed something feels heavier lately, and I don't want you carrying it alone."

Partner 1 (In distress):

"I'm just tired of being the f***ing problem. Honestly, it'd be better if I wasn't here. Everyone would be better off."

Partner 2 (Stays grounded, calm):

"I'm really glad you said that out loud. I need to ask you directly, because you matter to me. Are you thinking about suicide?"

Partner 1 (Quiet pause):

"I don't know ... sometimes I just want it all to stop. I'm so tired."

Partner 2:

"Okay. You're not alone in this. I'm not going to leave you hanging. Let's walk this together. This is a red flag for me, and I'm going to call in backup—because you deserve support that works. We're not pushing this off. We're getting help now."

Peer Supporter Action—Follow the Red Flag Flowchart:

- Confirm immediate safety (Are they alone? Access to means?).

- Activate your crisis protocol: commanding officer, agency MHP, chaplain, or 988.

- Stay with them or ensure they are not alone until help is secured.

- Afterward, connect with someone on your peer support team for your own processing and mental wellness.

Us: Roundtable Reflection

Reflect as a group on what it is like responding to a crisis involving one of your crewmates or a fellow peer supporter. This conversation is about getting honest with yourselves and one another. Validate any strong emotions that may have bubbled up for your peer support team.

Facilitator Instructions: After practicing the role-play, gather your peer supporters. Facilitate an open, structured reflection to debrief the partner practice.

Prompt: Partner 1s Reflect

- *"What was it like to share something that vulnerable? Did you feel heard, cared for, not alone?"*

- *"What would have helped even more in that moment?"*

Prompt: Partner 2s Reflect:

- *"What felt solid in your response?"*

- *"What was uncomfortable?"*

- *"What was it like saying the words out loud: 'Are you thinking about suicide?'"*
  (Did your chest tighten? Did your mind go blank? Or did you feel focused and clear?)

Group Exercise:

Facilitator goes around the circle pointing and looking at each peer supporter. Taking turns one by one, each peer supporter makes eye contact with the facilitator and clearly says out loud:

"Are you thinking about suicide?"

No softening. No euphemisms. Say it like someone's life depends on it—because sometimes, it does.

This exercise might feel uncomfortable or stir up strong emotions. That's the point. Just like drills *before* you hit the fireground, this training is meant to create stress and test your reactions. Practicing now, when the pressure is low, builds the muscle memory you will need when the stakes are high.

In the next chapter, you will expand your list of backup support—chaplains, vetted MHPs, 988, and peer support leaders with more advanced training or experience.

PART THREE:

Staying in the Fight

"Courage doesn't always roar. Sometimes it's the
quiet voice at the end of the day saying,
'I will try again tomorrow.'"

— Mary Anne Radmacher

---

(7)

IT'S NOT ALL
ON YOU

YOU ARE NOT SUPPOSED TO carry it all. Being a peer supporter does not mean you have to be the "fixer." You are not expected to be a therapist, a crisis counselor, or a savior. You are the bridge—not the endpoint. Your role is to listen, guide, and when needed, connect the person to a higher level of support. That next step could save a life.

When to Bring in the Pros

Certain cues indicate when it is time to call in a mental health professional. You will want to loop them in when:

- **Risk is high** (suicidal thoughts, self-harm, addiction relapse, domestic violence, or severe emotional distress).

- **You feel out of your depth**—trust that feeling, and don't wait.

- **The person needs more than you can offer** and is open to more support.

- The emotional weight of the role is **starting to wear on you**.

When in doubt, loop in a professional. Early. Quietly. Respectfully.

Whom You Call Matters

Your crews deserve more than a dusty EAP number. Build a trusted list of culturally competent mental health professionals. Look for those who understand fire service culture—not just general "first responder" work. As you decide whom to call, keep a few important things in mind:

✓ **Mental Health vs. Behavioral Health**

- Behavioral Health is a component of the broader Mental Health Continuum of Care. It focuses on stress responses, substance use, and coping behaviors. It often focuses on how *thoughts and behaviors* impact well-being.

- Mental Health covers the full continuum—prevention, trauma recovery, diagnosis, treatment, and long-term resilience. It addresses the underlying *psychological and emotional* challenges that drive behaviors.

You are looking for **professionals who understand the operational demands and cumulative stress of the fire service** (vs. general "first responder" culture).

✓ How to Vet a Clinic or Therapist

For tips on vetting a therapist, see the Appendix for a downloadable PDF of Chapter 22 from *Cover My Six: A Comprehensive Guide to Firefighter Care.*

When choosing or recommending a provider, consider:

1. Cultural Fit

- Do they have **real-world experience** with first responders? And do they understand the unique traits that set firefighters apart from other first responder groups?

- Have they spent time in a **firehouse** or do they understand how firefighters decompress after a call—*away* from public eyes?

- Do they speak "firefighter"? Can they keep up with the firehouse language and acronyms? If a counselor does not understand your shorthand way of speaking, you may end up spending more time in session explaining, rather than dealing with the presenting problem.

- Have they ever been **on scene**? Do they know the sights, sounds, and smells of a critical incident?

2. Clinical Competence

- Are they **licensed** and specialized in trauma, grief, or crisis response?

- Do they understand **the ripple effects**—how one firefighter's wellness affects crew, shift, family, and agency?

- Do they treat firefighter clients **as people**, no heroes? *Hero worship* in therapy undermines the firefighter's ability to focus on their own needs.

3. Availability & Communication

- Do they offer **flexible hours** that fit rotating shift work?

- Can they respond to **emergent needs** (outside typical 9–5 business hours)?

- What's their policy for **between-session contact**? Is it HIPAA compliant?

4. Confidentiality & Documentation

- Do they **understand firehouse confidentiality** and what "stays in the bay"?

- Can they explain how they **document sessions**, especially for those using insurance?

Note: Documentation matters—especially for those who own firearms. Clinical notes can affect careers. Ask about their documentation policies up front.

✓ **Trust Your Gut**

If most answers to the above are "no," **keep looking**. Many therapists offer **free phone consultations**. Take advantage of it. Firefighters and medics have sharp instincts for authenticity—**you will feel it when they get it**. If they do, make the appointment.

✓ **Keep the List Current**

An outdated list is a useless one. At least once a year:

- **Confirm contact info** (phone, email, websites)

- **Verify availability** (Are they still taking new clients? Do they accept insurance?)

- **Gather feedback** from peers who have used them.

- Assign someone in your department or union to **manage this task—** rotate responsibility to prevent burnout.

✓ **How to Make a Warm Handoff**

A **warm handoff** means you walk with them, not just point them in a direction. It might sound like:

> "Would it help to talk to someone who deals with this kind of thing every day? I know someone solid, and I can connect you."

Offer to call together, share contact info, or check in afterward. Stay connected through the process. That follow-up builds trust and helps them land on solid ground.

✔ **Resource List Tip**

Keep space in your workbook or team binder for a **Local & National Resources Page**: (to start, see References section at the back of this workbook).

- National Suicide & Crisis Lifeline: 988

- IAFF Center of Excellence

- Safe Call Now

- Local culturally competent clinicians/therapists/counselors (these are interchangeable titles for the same role)

- Department chaplain, critical incident team, or psychologist

Keep it accessible, updated, and visible. And remember—**you don't have to do this alone either.**

Me: It's Really Not All on Me

This section is for you—**20–30 minutes** of no judgment; just a chance to take stock of where you stand today. Being aware of your own beliefs, reactions, and inner hesitations will make you a stronger, steadier support for others.

✎ **How do I feel about breaking confidentiality in order to bring in backup support?** (Check in with your gut. Is there discomfort? Guilt? Relief? Fear of diminishing trust?)

_____

_____

_____

✎ **What biases or assumptions can I identify that I have today about mental health professionals (MHPs) or other community resources?**

(Think about past experiences, cultural messages, or department-wide attitudes that shaped your view.)

_____

_____

_____

✎ **How do I feel about handing someone over to an MHP?** (Does it feel like a failure? A relief? Do you wonder if it makes you seem weak or incapable?)

_____

_____

_____

✎ **What would it say about me if I let go of control and trusted someone else to help?** (This one digs deep. Sometimes we struggle to hand off because we feel responsible for the outcome.)

_____

_____

_____

Final Thought

You are not letting anyone down by passing the torch to a trained professional. You are doing your job as a peer supporter. Knowing when to call for backup is what keeps the whole crew strong.

You: The Warm Handoff

This **20-30-minute** exercise helps you get comfortable with making a warm handoff when things are above your pay grade. As a peer supporter, you are not supposed to carry it all—sometimes the best move you can make is connecting a brother or sister to the right kind of help, at the right time.

Scenario:

Partner 1 is in **acute distress**—they may be expressing suicidal thoughts, engaging in high-risk substance use, or showing clear signs of spiraling. They have not yet reached out for help. They are opening up a little but still minimizing or deflecting.

Partner 2 is the **peer supporter**, practicing how to recognize the red flags, affirm their role as support—not savior—and guide the person toward professional help with care and respect.

Instructions:

1. Take turns playing **Partner 1** and **Partner 2**.

2. Keep the tone real and respectful—not polished, not clinical.

3. Use direct questions, C.A.R.E. language, and stay calm under emotional pressure.

4. Aim to *make a warm handoff*—get agreement from Partner 1 that involving a professional is the next best step.

Practice Script:

Partner 1 (in acute distress): Say something like this but in your own words.

"I've just been trying to keep my head above water, but it's getting harder. Honestly, I've had a few nights where I thought about just disappearing. Nobody would notice anyway. And yeah, I've been drinking more, but whatever—it's just how I deal."

Partner 2 (peer supporter):

✓ Pause and **ground yourself**

✓ Use **Tactical Listening**

✓ Use **direct language** and **validation**

Try something like this (and put it into words comfortable for you):

"Thanks for trusting me with that. I can hear how heavy this is getting. You matter more than you think—you are not invisible."

"When you say stuff like 'disappearing' and drinking more to cope, that tells me we're at a point where more support is needed. This is above my pay grade, and I don't want to guess wrong with your life."

"Let's bring someone in who knows how to handle this. Not instead of me—alongside me. I'm not going anywhere, but I can't do this alone, and neither should you."

"I know someone who works with people in this exact kind of situation—first responders, real-life stuff. We can call together. Or I can text them while we sit here. You don't have to say a word yet. Can I do that for us?"

Debrief Questions—Debrief for **5 minutes** with your partner.

- How did it feel to say, "This is above my pay grade"?

- Did Partner 1 resist or push back? What helped shift the conversation?

- What language helped make the handoff feel like a team effort—not a rejection or abandonment?

- What could you each do better next time?

Us: Brainstorming for Backup

This **20–30-minute** discussion is designed to get your peer support team thinking together about trusted, vetted resources in your area. Chances are, between all of you, there's already a solid foundation of referral options—you just need to connect the dots.

Facilitator Instructions: Invite open (but voluntary) sharing.

Group Prompts:

- *"What came up for you during the warm-handoff partner exercise?"*

- *"What was **hard** about convincing someone to accept more help?"*

- *"What felt **natural or surprisingly easy** in the conversation?"*

- *"How do you personally feel about handing someone off to a mental health professional? What did that bring up about your own beliefs or fears?"*

- *"What does a **successful** warm handoff look like in our context?"*

- *"What **biases or assumptions** do we still carry about mental health professionals or clinics?"*

- *"What **bad experiences** have shaped how we view 'outside help'?"*

- *"What do we fear it says about **us** if we admit we cannot handle it alone?"*

Facilitator Tip: Normalize any discomfort—handing someone off does not mean giving up; it means playing your role with wisdom.

Group Activity: On a whiteboard, make two columns:

Our Trusted Resources

Whom do we already trust to call when the wheels come off?

Prompt ideas:

- Local therapists with first-responder experience

- Peer support team leads

- IAFF or department-based behavioral health partners

- Safe Call Now / 988 / Local crisis lines

- Department chaplains

- Veteran or military-informed clinicians

Still Need to Vet

Who's *on our radar* but we're not sure if they're the right fit yet?

Prompt ideas:

- Substance use treatment centers (e.g., center of excellence)

- New therapists recommended by someone, but we haven't checked them out yet

- Community clinics that advertise first-responder services

Assign Ownership for Updates

Ask:

- Who updates our resource list?

- How often do we review it?

- Who can test-drive some of these unknown resources and give feedback?

- Who wants to take the lead on cleaning up and organizing our go-to list?

Note: Rotate responsibility if possible. One person should not carry the entire system alone.

Wrap-Up Prompt

"What's one thing you want to remember or apply from today's conversation?"

Let everyone respond with a single sentence or phrase.

(8)

YOUR MENTAL ARMOR

IN THIS LINE of work, you would never head into a fire without your gear. Helmet. Turnouts. SCBA. Every piece has a purpose. Same goes for your mental armor. It is not about bubble baths and good vibes—it's about the daily tools that keep your mind sharp and clear under pressure.

Self-help strategies are your first tier of defense in your mental wellness regimen. They are <u>not</u> about waiting until things fall apart. They <u>are</u> about keeping you steady and prepared. What separates self-help from other strategies? These tools are **self-directed**. No one is going to do them for you, and you do not need a professional to start. You just need a decision: *I am going to take care of my mind like I do my gear—with intention, every day.*

Let's break it down.

Sleep Hygiene: Protecting Your Recovery Time

Sleep quality is a complex health concept made up of several distinct factors. Although it's not easily defined, the National Institutes of Health (U.S. Department of Health & Human Services) recognizes quality sleep as just as essential to human survival as food and water.[23,24] Over time, poor sleep habits and disrupted circadian rhythms significantly raise the risk of negative health outcomes and chronic diseases.[25] Beyond impacting overall health and well-being, research also suggests that sleep plays a critical role in maintaining cognitive function and workplace productivity.[26]

Sleep is not optional, especially for firefighters. It is the foundation your brain needs to process stress, stabilize mood, and regulate memory. Inconsistent sleep puts you at higher risk for anxiety, irritability, poor judgment, and long-term health issues.[27]

Tactics:

- Set a wind-down routine: same time, same order, every night.

- Block blue light 1 hour before bed (use amber glasses or night mode).

- Cool, dark room. 65°–68°F is ideal.

- Limit caffeine after 1300 hours (1:00 PM).

- If your schedule is chaotic, protect the hours you *do* get with blackout curtains and a sleep mask.

- Practice Yoga Nidra.*

* In a randomized controlled trial of patients with chronic insomnia, Yoga Nidra was associated with reduced cortisol levels and improvements in total sleep time, total wake time, and overall sleep quality.[28]

Quick Check:

☐ I shut down screens before bed.

☐ After night shifts, I prioritize sleep over household chores.

☐ I practice Yoga Nidra.

Exercise: Burn Off the Static

Physical movement resets your nervous system. When adrenaline builds up after a call—or stays stuck in your system from accumulated stress—movement helps burn it off. Regular exercise is a powerful tool for managing stress—helping regulate cortisol and adrenaline while boosting endorphin release, which enhances mood and reduces anxiety.[29] When a firefighter moves their body after a call, it helps the nervous system reset to baseline—instead of letting adrenaline and cortisol accumulate.

Tactics:

- Use short bursts: 15–20 minutes of HIIT (high-intensity interval training), kettlebell swings, or sprints.

- Walk it out: even 10 minutes post-call can lower cortisol.

- Train functionally: carry heavy stuff, climb stairs, simulate the job.

- Stack habits: listen to a podcast or audiobook while you move.

Quick Check:

☐ I get at least 20 minutes of movement 3–5 times a week.

☐ I use physical activity to decompress after high-stress calls.

☐ I view exercise as a mental reset, not just a physical task.

Nutrition: Fuel, Not Filler

You would never put bad diesel in an engine and expect it to run. Same goes for your brain. Your body uses what you eat to make stress hormones, repair tissues, and regulate your mood.[30] Vitamin and mineral supplementation plays a key role in optimizing health and has been shown to reduce perceived stress, anxiety, fatigue, and confusion.[31]

Tactics:

- Prioritize protein with every meal (eggs, lean meats, Greek yogurt).

- Cut back on sugar, soda, energy drinks, and ultra-processed foods. They spike your blood sugar, which then crashes, leaving you drained.

- Hydrate. Dehydration increases fatigue, confusion, and poor decision-making.

- Supplement your diet with vitamins and minerals.

Quick Check:

☐ I eat meals that include protein, carbs, and healthy fats.

☐ I hydrate consistently throughout my shift.

☐ I limit energy drinks and processed snacks.

☐ I consistently take vitamins and minerals as supplementation.

Cold-Water Immersion: Reset Your System

Cold-water immersion (CWI) is not a trend—it's a science-backed way to shift your nervous system. When done safely, it can reduce inflammation, boost mood, and improve stress resilience.[32] One study found that right after the cold plunge, **all negative emotional states dropped**, and **vigor increased**, with elevated mood persisting up to **24 hours later**.[33]

Tactics:

- Start small: 30-second cold shower at the end of your normal shower.

- Work up to 2–3 minutes of cold exposure, 3–4 times per week.

- Focus on breath: slow inhales and long exhales while in the cold.

- Avoid when sick, injured, or medically contraindicated.

Quick Check:

☐ I have tried cold exposure safely and with breath control.

☐ I use CWI to help downshift after mentally heavy shifts.

☐ I track how it affects my mood and recovery.

Self-Compassion: Not Weak, Just Real

The fire service trains you to be tough—and that's necessary. But toughness without care traps the damage inside. Self-compassion is a protecting agent for first responders.[34] It means treating yourself like you would treat a struggling crewmate—with **respect**, **understanding**, and **empathy**. Build your bounce-back muscle, <u>not</u> your inner critic.

Tactics:

- Talk to yourself like someone you respect. Ditch the "suck it up" message and replace it with "I'm having a hard time, and that's okay."

- Recognize mistakes without self-attack. "I dropped the ball on that call. I will fix it and keep going."

- Connect to humanity with phrases like "Struggle is a part of being human and I am not alone." This helps remind yourself that you are human, imperfect, and capable of growth.

Quick Check:

☐ I check my inner voice after a tough day.

☐ I allow space for struggle without judging it as a weakness.

☐ I show myself the same compassion I show others.

Mindfulness: Training for Your Attention

Mindfulness enhances firefighter resilience.[35] Mindfulness is not about clearing your head. It is about learning to *ground* and *notice*—your thoughts, your breath, your reactions, your emotions—without getting yanked around by them. It's tactical awareness for the inside of your brain.

Tactics:

- Box breathing: Inhale 4, hold 4, exhale 4, hold 4. Repeat 3–5 times.

- Mindful minutes: one minute of noticing what you see, hear, feel, smell, and taste, or focus on your breath.

- Do it in the rig, the shower, or the weight room—anywhere.

- Use an app like Calm, or fire-specific options like those found in the Cover My Six Newsletter: https://drleasullivan.systeme.io/newsletter

Quick Check:

- ☐ I have tried breathwork to reset after stress.

- ☐ I use brief moments of mindfulness daily.

- ☐ I can spot when I'm stuck in my head, and I shift to noticing my body easily.

Gear Up Daily

Mental armor only works if you put it on. None of these self-help tools are silver bullets. But together, they form a reliable shield. One that keeps you operational. One that helps you show up for others without losing yourself in the process.

Pick one strategy this week. Practice it like it's a turnout drill. Then add another. Over time, these habits become part of your baseline of readiness.

You do not need to be perfect. You just need to stay proactive—mind, body, and mission aligned.

Me: Check Your Gear

What's Working? Take **20–30 minutes** to consider the following.

Which self-care tools do you already use regularly, and what impact do they have? (Examples: "I get 7 hours of sleep on nights off." "Lifting after shift helps me shake off stress." "I cut down on caffeine and feel less jittery.")

✎ **Write 2–3 things that are working for you right now:**

_____

_____

_____

Where's the Weak Spot in Your Armor?

Every firefighter has a weak point. What is one habit you tend to drop when things get hectic? Where do you feel the effects most?

✎ **Write one area that needs attention:**

_____

✎ How does this impact your energy, mood, or focus?

_____

Choose Your Next Move

Pick **one** self-help tool from this chapter that you want to build into your routine. Don't overthink it—go for the one that feels _most doable right now._

☐ Sleep hygiene   ☐ Cold-water immersion

☐ Exercise   ☐ Self-compassion

☐ Nutrition   ☐ Mindfulness

✎ My next move is:

_____

_____

_____

✎ Here's when, where, and how I'll do it:

Example: "I will start adding cold-water exposure for 30 seconds at the end of my morning shower on A-shift days."

_____

_____

_____

Accountability Check

Who on your crew, in your circle, or at home can help you stick with this? (Not to nag you—but to remind you that you are not doing this alone.)

✎ **Name one person you will tell about your plan:**

_____

You: I've Got Your Six

In the fire service, you do not enter a structure alone—and you do not come out alone either. Your mental armor is also strongest when you pair self-accountability with support from someone who gets it. This **20–30-minute** exercise is meant to be done with a partner, building strength and connection for both of you.

Step 1: Compare Your Self-Care Toolkits

- Which tool comes easiest for you? Why?

- Which one feels hardest to stick with?

Step 2: Spot the Signals

Instructions:

Talk through the signs that you or your partner might need a reset. These are early indicators that your armor might be taking hits.

(Examples: "When I stop working out, it usually means I'm overloaded." "If I start skipping meals, I'm probably not doing great." "When I snap fast, I haven't slept or recovered from the last shift.").

✎ **Write down 2–3 personal warning signs for each of you:**

Name	Early Warning Signs
	_____
	_____
	_____
Me	_____
	_____
	_____
Partner	_____
	_____
	_____

Step 3: Hold the Line

Instructions:

Choose one **shared goal** this week. You each pick the same self-care tool to work on (e.g., better sleep, hydration, 3 cold showers, 2 workouts).

✎ **This week's shared focus is:**

_____

_____

_____

✎ **What our success looks like:**

_____

_____

_____

Example: "We both get 3 workouts in this week—even if it's just 20 minutes." "We both cut caffeine after 1300."

At the end of the week, text or tell each other:

"I held the line" or "I need a reset."

Step 4: Set a Weekly Check-in

Instructions:

Decide when and how you will check in with each other. It can be casual—but it has to be consistent. This is your peer support version of "accountability without judgment."

Examples:

- Text every Sunday night: "What's your win this week? What's your struggle spot?"

- Midweek check-in over coffee: "Still hitting your sleep goal?"

- After shift: "Did you use any of your tools today?"

Complete your plan below.

✎. **Our Check-In Plan:**

- Day & Time:

- Method (text, call, in person):

- Accountability Prompt:

"What's working? What's slipping? What's your next move?"

Final Reminder:

You drill together. You fight fire together. You recover together.

Accountability is not pressure—it's **protection**. Gear up. Check in. And definitely, do not go it alone.

Us: Our Mental Armor

This exercise gets your peer support team talking about what's holding strong in their own mental armor, what helps them reset, and how you can keep each other dialed in and accountable. After the partner practice, bring the whole group back together for a **20–30-minute** roundtable discussion.

Facilitator Prompt (put this into your own words):

- *"If your SCBA was down 30%, would you risk it—or swap it out?"*

- *"What's one sign your mental oxygen tank is running low?"*

(Examples: short fuse, skipping meals, waking up tired, avoiding people)

Pick 3–4 questions. Let the crew or peer support team talk—this isn't a checklist.

1. *"What part of your mental armor is strongest right now?"*
   → *"What habit do you hold onto when things get chaotic?"*

2. *"What slips first when you are overloaded?"*
   → *"How do you know it's slipping?"*
   → *"What would help protect it?"*

3. *"Gut check: How do you feel about the term 'self-compassion'?"*
   → *"Ever give someone grace you would not give yourself?"*

4. *"What's helped you reset—cold plunges, breathwork, sleep, something else?"*
   → *"What worked, what didn't, and what makes it easier to follow through?"*

5. *"How do we keep each other accountable without sounding like therapists?"*
   → *"What kind of check-in would actually fly with your crew?"*

Closing Prompt (use words most comfortable for you):

"Your gear fails without maintenance—so does your mindset. Mental armor is personal, but we can train for it together. That's what staying operational looks like—on shift and off."

Facilitator Option: As a peer support team, try the Audio Grounding Exercise: Hold the Line. Facilitator can play the guided exercise while the team practices mindfulness. Available for free download here:

https://drleasullivan.systeme.io/the-playbook-companion

(9)

HITTING TOO CLOSE TO HOME

EVERY FIREFIGHTER has a call that sticks. Sometimes it is the scene itself—too familiar, too raw. Sometimes it's what another responder shares, and suddenly your own stuff bubbles up.

When a call or someone else's experience hits too close to home, it is not about weakness. It is about being human in a high-impact role. The key is not to avoid these moments—they are inevitable as a peer supporter. The key is to prepare for them like you would any fireground risk—with a solid plan, the right tools, and trusted backup.

Whether or not you have already got your Mental Health Preplan in place (see Chapter 23 of *Cover My Six*), this workbook is here to help you take the next step—figuring out when a call hits too close to home and building your own backup crew and peer plan. This chapter will walk you through this vital preparation, so you are not caught off guard when the job brushes up against your own life.

Tactical Truth: Preparation Wins

On the fireground, the best outcomes follow a strong preplan. You think through worst-case scenarios, assign roles, and bring in the right equipment. Mental health is no different.

Too often, we wait until the wheels come off to ask for support—like figuring out your bailout plan *after* the floor gives way. When you know what trips your internal tones and have a plan ready, you are more likely to stay in control when the call hits close to home.

Recognize the Warning Signs

Before you can respond well, you have got to know the signs that *something is not sitting right*. When a call, something at home, or someone else's story, hits too close to home, it does not always announce itself clearly. Sometimes it creeps in. Other times it knocks you sideways.

Here's what it might look like:

- **A sudden emotional reaction on scene**
  You find yourself choking up, angry, overwhelmed, or disconnected from out of nowhere. Maybe you push it down because you are at shift, but it lingers afterward.

- **Intrusive memories from your own life**
  Something about the call echoes a personal trauma or painful

experience—past loss, childhood abuse, a friend's overdose, your own accident. Suddenly, you are reliving it.

- **Avoidance or irritation after a call**
  You snap at your crew, pick a fight at home, or shut down entirely. Maybe you don't want to talk about the call—or anything at all.

- **Sleep and focus take a hit**
  You cannot shut your brain off, or you keep seeing pieces of the call when you try to sleep. You're distracted, foggy, or keyed up during your off days.

- **Strong identification with the patient or their family**
  You start thinking, "That could've been my kid," "That's just like my brother," or "This feels way too familiar." You are carrying their pain like it's yours.

These signs do not mean you are weak. They do not mean you are broken. They mean you have encountered a **high-impact stressor**—and your system is doing what it was designed to do: *respond*.

This is your cue. When you notice these reactions, it is not a red flag—it's an *early warning system*. And that is when you turn to your Mental Health Preplan.

✎. Take a moment to identify and describe what it looks like when a call hits too close to home for you:

_____

_____

_____

Bring in Your Backup

In this line of work, you do not approach a scene alone. Not on the fireground, not on a tough EMS call, not when conditions are unstable. When the risk goes up, you call for backup—*because your life could depend on it.*

Your **mental and emotional health** deserves the same strategy.

When a call hits too close to home, it can throw you off balance *fast*. You may feel overwhelmed, shut down, or tempted to tough it out solo. But just like in the field, going it alone is dangerous. You need a plan for whom to call in when the pressure is too high to manage on your own.

Think of it this way:

- **On scene:** You size up hazards and assign roles.

- **Mentally:** You size up your stress load and assign support.

This is not about being weak—it's about being *smart*. A strong firefighter does not wait until they are trapped to ask for help. They plan and prepare for it ahead of time.

Who is in your mental backup crew when things get too real?

- A fellow peer supporter you trust to talk things through—someone in the job who "gets it" and can hold space without judgment.

- A mental health professional who understands the job— who knows fire service culture (how it's unique from other first responders) and doesn't need the acronyms explained.

- A chaplain or spiritual leader—who helps you process loss, moral injury, or meaning.

- A partner, sibling, or longtime friend outside the firehouse who knows you well—someone outside the job who knows who you are beyond the uniform.

You do not need to lean on all of them at once. One solid connection is a good start. **The key is having names and contact info ready before you need them.**

Do not rely on memory when your system is flooded. That is like trying to find your SCBA in a smoke-charged room—too late. You want support standing by.

Me: Build Your Backup Crew

Take **20–30 minutes** to identify your personal backup crew. These are the people you trust to show up when you are struggling—without needing to fix you.

✎ Write their names, roles, and how you will reach them:

- **Peer Supporter / Trusted Co-worker**

  Name:

  Best way to reach:

- **Mental Health Professional**

  Name:

  Contact info:

- **Spiritual Support (Chaplain, Faith Leader)**

  Name:

  Contact info:

- **Personal Support (Partner, Family, Friend)**

  Name:

  Best way to reach:

Tactical Tip:

Post this list where you will see it—your locker or turnout bag or saved in your phone under "Mental Backup." The goal is fast access, not a scavenger hunt when your head is not clear.

When things get heavy, do not hesitate. Call them in. That is not overreacting. That's doing what trained professionals do: **protect the asset—** and in this case, *you* are the asset.

You: Creating a Peer Plan

This **20–30-minute** partner practice is about sharpening your peer support skills by getting real about your own stress signals—and helping each other build action plans you can actually use in the moment. It is easier to stay ahead of the curve when you have someone in your corner, ready to go, who knows what to look for and how to respond.

Step 1: Choose Your Partner

Pick someone you trust—another firefighter, peer supporter, or someone from your station or crew who knows you well. This works best with someone who has seen you on and off duty.

Step 2: Take Turns Sharing

Each person answers the following out loud, one at a time. The other person listens without interrupting or problem-solving. (Write down your partner's responses to help you remember their stress cues.)

✎ **When a call hits too close to home, here's how my partner tends to react:**

- Emotionally (e.g., anger, withdrawal, sadness):

  _____

  _____

  _____

- Physically (e.g., tension, fatigue, restlessness):

  _____

  _____

  _____

- Behaviorally (e.g., isolating, snapping, avoiding calls):

_____

_____

_____

✎. Here's how they usually try to cope—whether or not it works:

_____

_____

_____

_____

_____

_____

✎. Here's what they want me to do if I notice they are struggling:

- What *helps*:

- What *does not help*:

Step 3: Create a Peer Plan

Now each of you writes down a short action plan for how you will back the other person up when they hit a tough call or personal trigger.

✎ **If I see my partner struggling, here's how I'll show up:**

- What I'll say or ask:

- What I'll *avoid* saying:

- How I'll follow up:

Agree on a simple check-in system (text, walk, phone call, gym meet-up, etc.). You do not need to be their therapist—you are their backup.

Step 4: Final Debrief (2 Minutes Each)

Take turns answering:

- What is one thing you learned about yourself through this?
- What is one thing you are committing to try next time a call hits close to home?

Us: When the Call Hits Home

This **30–40-minute** group exercise will help normalize real conversations about the emotional impacts of shift work in EMS, identify common stress signals, and encourage proactive planning and peer support.

Facilitator Role: Guide the flow, model honest (not perfect) responses, and ensure psychological safety. Participation is encouraged, not required.

Facilitator Opener (change it to your own meaningful words):

"We all have calls that hit harder than others—ones that mirror our own lives or open up old wounds. This discussion is not about therapy or fixing anyone. It's about being real, being prepared, and knowing how to back each other up when things get personal. Let's talk about what that actually looks like."

Prompt:

"What are some cues that a call—or someone else's story—is hitting too close to home for you? What do you notice in yourself or others when things get personal?"

Follow-ups:

- *"What do you tend to do or feel in those moments?"*

- *"How does your body usually let you know you are carrying something?"*

Facilitator Tips:

- Normalize a range of responses: shutdown, anger, irritability, reaching for carbs or alcohol, hyperfocus, etc.

- Share one of your own (briefly) to model honesty and vulnerability.

Prompt:

"Who is a part of your mental or emotional backup when things get rough? What kind of support actually works for you—or what would you want when you notice a stress signal?"

Follow-ups:

- *"What kind of check-in from a peer actually helps you?"*

- *"What would you want a crew member to avoid doing or saying?"*

Encourage clarity, not just theory. Help the group think through practical ideas.

Prompt:

"What is one thing you can add to your mental health preplan this week?"

(This could be a person to talk to, a specific coping strategy, or just naming a red flag they'll pay closer attention to.) Sharing these aloud as a group can help offer ideas that other peer supporters had not considered and may be able to use as part of their own preplan.

Facilitator Script (again, use words that feel comfortable to you):

"This job asks a lot. It's not weakness when something hits close to home—it's a sign you are still human. But just like we don't fight fire solo, we do not have to carry this stuff solo either. Keep your preplan close, know your backup, and check in with your people. We protect each other by staying ready and staying real."

PART FOUR:

Be the Culture You Want to See

"Alone we can do so little.
Together we can do so much."

— Helen Keller

---

(10)

COVERING THE CREW, BRIEFING THE BRASS

YOU ARE HERE for your crew—but the job does not stop at the bay doors. If you are serious about peer support, you have got to learn how to navigate leadership too.

It's a tricky line to walk: You want to have the backs of your brothers and sisters, but you also need the trust, resources, and buy-in from your officers and chiefs. And let's be real—many in the upper ranks did not grow up in a culture where talking about mental health was the norm. So how do you speak their language without selling out your crew?

This chapter is about exactly that: How to protect the people who confide in you *and* work effectively with leadership. It's not about politics—it's about doing the job right.

Trust Flows Both Ways: Holding the Line on Confidentiality

Confidentiality is the bedrock of any peer support program. If your crew suspects that what they share might end up on the chief's desk, they'll stop talking—and the program fails before it even starts.

Here's your anchor:

What is said in peer support stays in peer support, unless someone is a danger to themselves or others, or reports something that's required by law.

Your leadership needs to hear this *early and often*. Make it clear that peer support is not an intelligence-gathering operation. You're not reporting mood, behavior, or rumors—you're protecting psychological safety.

When leadership asks for "updates" on morale or individual members, here's what you can say instead:

"I can't speak to any individual's situation, but I can share that our crew is carrying a heavy load this season. We're seeing signs of cumulative stress. Our peer support team is active and engaged, and we're encouraging folks to use the tools we've trained in."

Stay general. Stay professional. Be honest without crossing the line.

Getting Buy-In Without Becoming the "Mental Health Guy"

Let's address the elephant in the room. Nobody wants to be *that guy*—the one leadership tolerates but crew members avoid. You didn't sign up to be a therapist. You signed up to make sure your people do not fall through the cracks.

So how do you talk to executive leadership in a way that gets real support for your team—without putting a target on your back?

Start by shifting the frame:

- You're not pushing a "mental health agenda."

- You're enhancing operational readiness and crew longevity.

- You're protecting the department's most valuable asset: its people.

Use their language. Chiefs want to know: *How does this help the mission? How does this reduce liability? What's the ROI?*

Try phrases like:

- *"This isn't therapy—it's tactical support that helps us keep our crews in the fight longer and safer."*

- *"Peer support helps us catch small problems before they become disciplinary issues or resignations."*

- *"This is about retention, morale, and making sure our firefighters can do the job and go home in one piece."*

The key is **showing the value**, not preaching the message.

Bringing in a Mental Health Professional as a Strategic Ally

One of the most effective ways to protect the integrity of peer support and maintain a healthy channel with leadership is to bring in a trusted, culturally competent **contracted mental health professional (MHP)**.

This professional is not there to replace peer support. They're there to **strengthen the system** by serving three key functions:

1. **Clinical backup** for cases that go beyond the peer support scope

2. **A liaison to leadership** who can speak to mental health trends without breaking confidentiality

3. **An advisor** who helps the peer support team stay grounded, supported, and trained

Having a designated MHP—someone who understands the fire service and has earned the trust of both crews and command—takes pressure off the peer support team. It allows you to stay in your lane while knowing someone is tracking the big picture.

How it helps leadership:

- They have a go-to professional who can speak in metrics and mitigation language

- It reduces liability by showing the department has real support systems in place

- It gives them confidence that someone is clinically monitoring the trends

How it helps you:

- You're not expected to carry everything

- You don't have to decode or translate clinical language for leadership

- You have a resource when a situation needs more than peer support can ethically provide

When used right, a contracted MHP becomes a **force multiplier**—bridging trust between union members and the executive level without compromising the core value of confidentiality.

Building Credibility Without Oversharing

If leadership does not understand what peer support is or how it works, they will be hesitant to back it. But they also do not need to hear confidential stories or emotional appeals. Instead, speak in **patterns and principles:**

"We've noticed increased sleep disruption and family strain after back-to-back structure fires. We're addressing it through check-ins and practical strategies like tactical decompression. The team is getting traction."

This shows that your program is active, responsive, and structured—all without compromising anyone's privacy.

Bonus tip: Bring short, written updates every quarter. Keep it high-level:

- Number of team activations (no names)

- Common themes (e.g., family stress, grief, burnout)

- Training hours logged

- Resources used or requested

This builds trust, shows accountability, and keeps peer support in the chain of communication—without breaching it.

Making Leadership Part of the Culture Shift

Buy-in is not a one-time conversation. It's a relationship.

If you can get even one key leader to understand and support the purpose of your team, you've got a foothold. From there, the goal is to embed peer support into the larger culture of leadership—not as an add-on, but as a leadership skill set.

Invite officers to observe parts of trainings (not sessions). Bring them in on the "why" behind what you do. Offer talking points they can use at briefings to reinforce the importance of looking out for one another.

And if you hit resistance? Stay steady. Your role is not to convince everyone. It's to do the work well enough that it cannot be ignored.

You're Not in This Alone

Remember: You are not the department therapist. You are not HR. And you are not a replacement for clinical care.

What you *are* is a **bridge**. A peer who understands the grind and can spot the signs before someone breaks. A steady voice who can talk to leadership *and* the line. A professional who knows that doing this right means balancing two priorities: **Protect your crew and keep command informed.**

That is how you cover the crew—and brief the brass.

Me: Leading Up Without Selling Out

Before you can speak with confidence to leadership, it helps to get clear on what you stand for—what you are protecting, what you are afraid of, and how you want to show up. This **10–15-minute** reflection is designed to ground you in your role as a peer supporter and clarify the values that guide your communication with command staff. Find a quiet place. Write honestly. No one else needs to see this but you.

✎ **When I talk to leadership about peer support, what do I feel confident about?**

What knowledge, experience, or values do I bring to the table that I trust?

_____

_____

_____

✎ What part of those conversations make me hesitate or hold back?

Is it fear of judgment? Not knowing the right words? Worry about being misunderstood?

_____

_____

_____

✎ What am I afraid that leadership will not "get" about peer support?

What's at risk if they don't understand? What assumptions do I think they might have?

_____

_____

_____

✎ What values do I want to protect when I speak on behalf of my fellow brothers and sisters?

Think about confidentiality, trust, operational readiness, or anything else that matters deeply to you.

_____

_____

_____

✎. **What is one message that I want to stand behind—no matter who I'm talking to?**

Write a sentence you believe in, something you'd be proud to say in any room.

_____

_____

_____

When you are clear on your role and grounded in your values, you can navigate the chain of command without losing your integrity—or your crew's trust. This is how strong peer support leaders are built: one honest conversation at a time, starting with yourself.

You: Rehearsing the Hard Conversations

This **20–30-minute** exercise is designed to help you practice holding the line on confidentiality with leadership while learning how to communicate in a way that builds trust and partnership—instead of tension or pushback.

Instructions:

Take turns practicing a short scenario where one of you plays the **Peer Support Lead** and the other plays the **Executive Officer or Battalion Chief**. Use the examples below. Rotate roles after each 5–10-minute round.

Scenario Examples:

1. **The Chief wants names:**
   "Can you tell me who's been struggling lately? We're hearing complaints and need to get ahead of it."

2. **Budget justification:**
   "You're asking for more training hours and resources. Why should we spend department funds on this instead of more equipment?"

3. **Crisis follow-up:**
   "After that rough structure fire, how are people doing? Are we at risk of losing anyone?"

4. **Dismissive leadership:**
   "We didn't have peer support back in my day, and we were fine. I think the crews just need to toughen up."

Your task as the peer supporter:
Practice responding in a way that—

- Protects confidentiality

- Reinforces the mission and value of peer support

- Uses operational language to communicate impact

- Holds your ground respectfully

Debrief after each round:

What worked? What felt forced? What language helped you hold the boundary of confidentiality? What would you do differently in a real conversation? How could you reframe your message to better align with leadership's priorities (retention, readiness, liability, etc.)?

Us: Speaking to Leadership

This **20–30-minute** exercise will help peer support team members reflect on what works—and what does not—when communicating with executive leadership, and to build confidence in using operational, boundary-respecting language.

Facilitator Notes:

- Keep the tone grounded and practical.

- Encourage supporters to be honest about their real challenges.

- Emphasize there are no perfect answers—this is about learning from each other.

Opening Prompt:

"When we talk to command staff or officers about peer support, we are walking a line: Protecting our people while earning leadership's trust. Let's talk about what helps us do that well—and where we can get better."

Discussion Questions:

- What phrases or approaches have helped you explain peer support to leadership—without crossing confidentiality lines?

  Encourage participants to share language that has worked or backfired.

- Have you ever felt pressured to give more information than you were comfortable with? How did you handle it—or how would you handle it next time?

- What concerns do you think executive leadership has about peer support programs? How can we address those concerns without selling out the crew?

- What do you think peer support leaders need to *sound like* or *act like* in front of command to gain credibility—without losing authenticity?

- What's one boundary you are committed to holding, even under pressure?

- What kind of support would help you feel more confident talking to leadership—training, scripting, mentorship, etc.?

Wrap-Up Prompt:

"Based on what we talked about today, what's one piece of language or one mindset shift you want to bring into your next leadership interaction?"

(11)

GROWING YOUR COMMUNITY

FIRE DOES NOT CARE about jurisdictional lines. When the call goes out, mutual aid is the name of the game. The same should be true when it comes to protecting the mental health and resilience of the people behind the turnout gear.

Too often, agencies operate in silos—each trying to patch together its own resources for mental health, peer support, and leadership buy-in. That approach not only burns time and energy but also limits what you can offer your crews. There is a smarter way forward: **build alliances with neighboring agencies**. When you work together, you build a force multiplier of care.

Here's how.

Form a Peer Support Consortium

Start by connecting peer support teams across agencies in your region.

A **peer support consortium** allows departments to:

- Cross-train together using shared language and tools

- Debrief large-scale incidents collaboratively (especially when multiple agencies are involved)

- Offer surge capacity when one agency's peer team is overwhelmed

- Swap lessons learned and stay updated on trends in responder wellness

This is more than mutual aid—it's mutual **resilience**. A firefighter might be more comfortable talking to a peer from another department, especially if they fear internal politics or confidentiality breaches. A regional network gives them options without leaving them stranded.

Action Step: Host a quarterly "Consortium Coffee" or working group— rotating locations—where peer leads from each agency can connect, compare protocols, and troubleshoot challenges.

Collaborate on Shared Behavioral Health Resources

No single district or department has all the answers—or all the providers. Pooling your vetted resources makes it easier for everyone to access solid, culturally competent care.

Share a vetted directory of:

- First-responder counselors (who specifically understand fire culture)

- Substance use treatment programs with first-responder tracks

- Chaplains or critical incident response team members trained in emergency services support

- Accelerated Resolution Therapy (ART) or Eye Movement Desensitization and Reprocessing (EMDR) providers familiar with cumulative trauma and critical incidents

When agencies collaborate, it is easier to negotiate memorandums of understanding (MOUs), co-host wellness trainings (including cost sharing), and build a stronger bench of backup support. You are also reducing wait times and improving care continuity when your members need a referral.

Action Step: Create a shared digital "Behavioral Health Resource Bank" accessible by peer team leads, chaplains, and wellness officers across agencies.

Contract a Culturally Competent Mental Health Professional (MHP)

Every agency should have at least one **designated contracted MHP**—a clinician who is more than trauma-informed. That experience alone does not cut it in this line of work.

© 2025 by Dr. Lea Sullivan

Firefighters need someone who understands fire service life. The impact of shift work. The dark humor. The minimizing of gruesome or dangerous as a "normal Monday". The sleep debt. The family strain. The moral injury. The heavy fear of being a burden. The ability to bond.

Without this baseline understanding, two things happen:

1. Firefighters waste time in therapy explaining how the job works instead of getting to what's weighing on them.

2. The therapist misses subtle cues, hesitates to go deep, or gives advice that flat out does not fit the culture.

When the right fit *is* in place, that provider becomes a trusted extension of the wellness team. They know how to ride the fine line between support and accountability, and they know when a client needs a sounding board versus a safety net.

Action Step: In consortium meetings, coordinate efforts to vet and contract with MHPs across agencies—ideally ones who already work with fire service personnel or are open to clinician ride-alongs and station visits to build credibility. On-scene experience is rare, but a huge therapeutic benefit to firefighter clients.

Final Thoughts: No Agency Stands Alone

If fire is a team sport, so is mental health. Building cross-agency community takes effort—but it pays off in trust, coverage, and lasting care.

Don't wait for the next critical incident to realize your peer team is maxed out or your provider list leads nowhere.

You've got mutual aid plans for structure fires—now build them for mental health.

Me: Mutual Aid for the Mind

Take **20–30 quiet minutes** to reflect on how your agency is currently engaging (or not engaging) with neighboring districts or departments around mental health and wellness. Use the prompts below to guide your thinking. Be honest. This is about readiness, not judgment.

✎ How connected is our agency with nearby departments when it comes to peer support or mental wellness?
(Are we operating in a silo? Are there regular conversations or joint efforts?)

_____

_____

_____

✎ Have I ever reached out to—or been reached out to by—a peer team member from another agency? What was the result?
(If not, why? If yes, what worked and what didn't?)

_____

_____

_____

✎ Do we have a trusted list of mental health resources we'd feel confident sharing with a neighboring department?
(Is that list up to date, culturally competent, and diverse enough to meet different needs?)

_____

_____

_____

✎. If a firefighter from my crew needed help tomorrow, do I have a go-to clinician I could refer them to who understands our world without needing a crash course in fire life?
(If not, what's the barrier? Access? Funding? Trust?)

_____

_____

_____

✎. What's one simple action I could take this month to strengthen cross-agency support in our region?
(Could be a phone call, a meeting invitation, sharing a resource, or suggesting a joint training.)

_____

_____

_____

Final Reflection:

Instead of competing with neighboring agencies, what if we joined forces? The strongest crews are not the ones who go it alone—they're the ones who train, show up, and have each other's backs. Imagine what we could build if we stopped guarding our turf and started guarding each other—across departments, across districts, as one fire family.

You: Mutual Aid Isn't Just for Fires

Now let's take **20–30 minutes** to explore ways your agency can connect with neighboring departments for mental wellness support—and identify one immediate action step. Partner up. You know the drill.

Instructions:

1. **Start with this question:**
   "What do you wish our agency had more of when it comes to mental health or peer support?"
   Take turns answering. Be specific—think counselors, CISM or debriefing help, chaplain support, etc.

2. **Now ask:**
   "Who nearby might already have that?"
   Consider which agencies, programs, or individuals in your region you might partner with or who have strengths you can learn from.

3. **Brainstorm together:**
   "What's one connection our agency could make this month to start building mutual support across department lines?"

   Examples:

   • Invite another department's peer support lead for a station visit

   • Co-host a mental health training

   • Share your vetted mental health resources list

   • Schedule a meet-and-greet with a first-responder chaplain or clinician (counselor/therapist/MHP)

4. **Make it real:**

Each partner writes down *one commitment* they'll follow through on in the next 30 days to strengthen cross-agency wellness. Share it out loud to your partner for accountability.

Us: Build a Bridge, Not a Wall

Take **20–30 minutes** as a group to identify gaps, share strengths, and generate regional strategies for collaborative mental wellness support across fire agencies.

Step 1: Scan the Horizon

Go around the room and have each participant respond briefly to the following prompt:

"What's one thing our agency does well in terms of peer support or mental wellness—and what's one area we are still trying to figure out?"

Encourage honesty without judgment. Capture themes on a whiteboard (e.g., "solid peer team," "need a vetted MHP," "no follow-up after major calls," etc.)

Step 2: Strengthen the Gaps

Facilitate a group discussion using these guiding questions:

- *"Where are we duplicating efforts that could be shared?"*

- *"What resources or clinicians do we already have access to that others might benefit from?"*

- *"Are there gaps that every agency here is struggling with? What could we build together to address those?"*

- *"If one agency was hit hard by a line-of-duty death or large-scale trauma, what plan is in place for peer support teams to help their neighbors? Do we need one?"*

Optional visual aid: Draw a simple map of local departments and sketch lines between them as people talk—highlighting where collaboration already exists and where it's needed.

Step 3: Take the First Step

End with clear action steps. One final prompt:

"What's one action we'll take in the next 30 days to strengthen our regional network?" (Examples: host a joint peer training, share MHP contact info, meet with a clinician as a group, propose an MOU, etc.)

Write each commitment down and circle back at the next quarterly meeting or check-in.

Closing Reflection (in your own words):

"The fireground teaches us to rely on mutual aid. Mental health should be no different. We may wear different patches—but we're all standing in the same heat."

(12)

SUSTAINING
THE MISSION

PEER SUPPORT IS NOT a one-off call or a short-term project. It's a mission—a way of leading with presence, with purpose, and with clarity. If you have made it through this workbook—and *Cover My Six: A Comprehensive Guide to Firefighter Care* before it—you have invested in something bigger than yourself. You have built skills, strengthened your crew, and set the foundation for a culture where asking for help is not weakness—**it's readiness**.

But now comes the most overlooked part of the job: **keeping it going**. Not just for the next month. For the next five, ten, twenty years.

Because the reality is this: Peer support is not a sprint. It's a long haul. And the only way to do it well—for the long run—is to be smart about how you build, rest, rotate, and reinforce your team.

Let's talk about how you can do that well.

Boundaries Keep the Mission Alive

The fastest way to lose good peer supporters is to push them until they burn out. And burnout does not always look like a breakdown—it can show up as numbness, irritability, detachment, or just checking out.

Sustainable peer support means having boundaries.

- You are not available 24/7.

- You are not the solution to every crisis.

- You're allowed to say, "I'm not the right fit for this one."

- You're allowed to take time off from the team.

Boundaries certainly are not weakness. **They're wisdom.** They keep the work honest, clear, and sustainable—for you and the people you serve.

It's Not "Once a Peer, Always a Peer"

Being selected for peer support is an honor—but it's not a life sentence. In fact, staying too long on the team without reflection can lead to compassion fatigue, tunnel vision, or a slow erosion of effectiveness.

Wise peer teams re-evaluate and rotate their members—on purpose.

- **Set term limits** (e.g., two years with an option to reapply).

- **Create off-ramps** that allow people to step back without shame or drama.

- **Make space for fresh eyes, new energy, and different strengths.**

- **Invite returning team members to help mentor the next round.**

The goal is not to keep everyone on board forever—it's to keep the team adaptable, trusted, and sharp.

Rotate Roles and Build Bench Strength

If only one or two people are handling all the calls, all the logistics, and all the emotional labor, the team is already at risk. Sustainability depends on **shared ownership.**

- Rotate leadership roles: Let others lead meetings, debriefs, or training efforts.

143

- Cross-train: Make sure everyone knows how to make referrals, document follow-ups, and connect with MHPs.

- Spot potential: Who on your crew shows natural peer support qualities but has not stepped up yet? Invite them to train.

Strong teams do not rely on heroes—they build a **system of strength**.

Celebrate the Wins—Especially the Quiet Ones

Peer support wins often happen behind the scenes:

"When you listened, I really felt understood. Thanks."

"I finally reached out to that counselor."

"Because of our debrief, that call didn't stick like it used to."

"I didn't feel alone this week."

If you wait for big saves to feel like you are making a difference, you will miss the real impact. The quiet moments *are* the mission.

- Acknowledge effort in team meetings.

- Debrief the positive, not just the painful.

- Say thank you. Especially to the peer who made the quiet check-in, the follow-up call, or the referral that no one else saw.

Recognition does not cost anything—but it fuels everything.

Keep Training and Stay Connected

Skills atrophy if you do not use them. And isolation—even on a peer support team—can lead to drift.

- **Train regularly.** Refresh your tools. Attend courses. Learn about suicide risk, addiction, grief, complex trauma, or moral injury.

- **Debrief as a team.** Make time for reflection—not just after hard calls, but as a rhythm of crew and peer supporter life.

- **Use your contracted MHP.** They should be more than a name on a list. Let them guide, consult, and challenge you when needed.

And remember—**peer supporters need support too.** Have each other's backs. Ask, "How are you doing?" and mean it.

Final Thoughts: This Is the Long Game

You have put in the reps. You've done the work. Now the mission is to keep it going—without losing yourself or burning out the people next to you.

This is the part most people skip over. But if you want your peer team to still be standing strong five years from now, this is the chapter that matters most.

So set your boundaries. Rotate your people. Celebrate your wins. Keep training. Step back when needed. Step up when called. And above all, keep building the kind of team that others know they can trust—because you all take care of yourself *and* your people.

The mission is worth it.
And so are you.

Me: Stronger Than I Started

This is where you take **20–30 minutes** to pause, take a breath, and look at the road ahead. You have added new tools. You have built trust with your peer support team. Now it's time to ask: *How do I keep doing this work well—without burning out, checking out, or trying to do it all alone?* Take your time. No one's grading this. This is for you.

✎ **What has changed in me since starting this workbook—or since stepping into peer support?**
(What have I learned about myself, my limits, my leadership, or my crew?)

_____

_____

_____

✎ **Who's on my bench?**
(Who can I mentor, train, or encourage to step up so I don't carry this alone?)

_____

_____

_____

✎. What would I call a "quiet win" in the last six months—and did I give it the credit it deserved?
(What felt meaningful, even if no one else saw it?)

_____

_____

_____

✎. What support do *I* need more of right now—and what's stopping me from asking for it?
(Who can I reach out to? What's one step I can take this week?)

_____

_____

_____

✎. Final Check-In

Complete the sentence below to express what feels most true for you right now:

• One boundary I will protect more clearly moving forward is:

_____

_____

_____

- One way I will keep the mission going *without burning out* is:

  _____

  _____

  _____

- One action I'll take this month to build up the team around me is:

  _____

  _____

  _____

Closing Thought:

You do not have to be perfect. **In fact, "perfection" is not a human experience.** You just have to be present, prepared, and willing to grow.

Stay in the fight—but don't lose yourself in it.

You are not in this alone.

You: Strong with You

Now, let's take **20–30 minutes** to reflect on individual and team sustainability. This exercise will help you identify real-world actions to protect each other and the mission going forward.

Step 1: Personal Inventory

Take turns answering these prompts out loud to your partner. Listen without fixing—this is about being heard, not being solved.

- *"What part of peer support work refuels me—and what part is starting to wear me down?"*

- *"What is one boundary that I need to hold better if I want to keep doing this well?"*

- *"What support do I wish I had more of—and where can I ask for it?"*

Step 2: Team Reality Check

Now shift focus from individual experience to team sustainability. Discuss:

- *"Are we rotating roles and responsibilities well—or are the same people always stepping up?"*

- *"Who on the team needs a break or a check-in?"*

- *"Who's a quiet strength that we should start mentoring for more responsibility?"*

✎ Write down any ideas worth bringing to your full team.

_____

_____

_____

Step 3: Make a Mutual Commitment

Each partner shares one commitment they'll act on in the next 30 days to protect their sustainability or build up the team. It might be:

- Setting a new boundary

- Checking in on another peer

- Mentoring someone new

- Taking a week off peer duties

- Starting a quiet celebration ritual (e.g., monthly "peer win" shout-outs)

✎ Write down your commitment here.

_____

_____

_____

Say your commitment out loud. Your partner's job is to *support*, not pressure.

Us: Strongest Together

As your final whole-group roundtable exercise, take 45–60 minutes to close the workbook journey with connection, a shared vision for long-term sustainability, and a final graduation ceremony.

Step 1: Real Talk

Go around the circle and have each person share a response to the following prompt:

> *"What's one thing I've learned—about myself, this work, or this team— that I want to carry forward from here?"*

Encourage people to keep it real. Vulnerability = trustworthiness. Humor and honesty are both welcome.

Step 2: The Five-Year Question

Wrap-Up Prompt:

> *"What systems or habits would make this team stronger in five years?"*

> *"What does it look like, for real? What do we look like as a peer support team five years from now?"*

Let this one go deep. Silence is okay. You are building something here.

Step 3: Celebrate the Wins

Graduation is not just the completion of training—it's the beginning of stepping into a role where your crew depends on you in a new way. A closing ritual marks that transition, honors the work you have done, and reminds the team of the mission ahead.

Your ritual does not need to be formal. What matters is that it **feels authentic to your team** and sends a clear message: *we're in this together, and we're ready to serve.*

Here are some ideas to spark your own tradition:

- **Shared phrase**: End by speaking a line together that captures your commitment (e.g., "I've got your six").

- **Symbolic gesture**: A handshake or fist bump passed around the circle.

- **Marking the shift**: Ringing a bell, handing out challenge coins, rocker patches, or lapel pins to signify stepping into service.

- **One-word sendoff**: Each member shares a single word for how they're leaving this training.

- **Gratitude round**: Everyone names one strength they see in the team moving forward.

Remember: the ritual is less about the "what" and more about the **shared meaning**. Pick something that your team can repeat every time you welcome in new peer supporters. That consistency will anchor the training as more than just a class—it becomes a tradition.

Final Words (in your own comfortable tone, of course):

"Graduation is not the finish line—it's the starting line. Look around this circle. These are the people you will lean on, and the ones leaning on you. You do not have to carry it all. We carry it together. That's what makes this team different. Today, we step forward with new skills, but more importantly, with a stronger bond. Let's carry that with us from this day forward. Now, let's get to work."

Congratulations

from Dr. Lea

DEAR PEER SUPPORTER,

Congratulations on completing this playbook! You've stepped into one of the most demanding and meaningful roles in the fire service: standing steady for a brother or sister when they can't stand on their own. This role demands grit, humility, and compassion.

There will be times when a crewmate reaches out in the middle of the night. A mental health professional can listen, but they are not a peer. They do not carry the bond of the firehouse, the lived experience of the job, or the trust that comes from walking side by side on calls. That lane belongs to you—and it's powerful. You bring a balance of skills and camaraderie that no MHP can replicate. That's the heart of peer support.

The truth is, what you're doing matters more than you may ever realize. The quiet check-ins, the willingness to ask the hard question, the simple act of refusing to let someone walk through pain alone—these moments save lives and change the fire service for the better.

Never underestimate the impact of what you do.

I am proud of the work you have put in here. You've earned the right to be called a Peer Supporter. Carry that title with courage, humility, and respect. Your presence is a lifeline—and your team is stronger because of you.

Hold the line. Cover each other's six. And remember—you are never standing alone.

In your corner,

Lea

RESOURCES

———

Tough Minds www.toughminds.org/crisis-plan

Our tools aim to arm everyone with real resources to manage their own mental health, from the day-to-day to crisis moments. Using AI and tech, we're building a suite of tools that help people plan ahead, stay steady in tough moments, and build emotional resilience skills through training. Our tools are forever free with no data collection, and shared by counselors, charities and schools.

Safe Call Now: 206-459-3020

This confidential, comprehensive 24/7 crisis referral service is for all public safety employees and all emergency services (EMS) personnel and their family members nationwide.

National Suicide and Crisis Lifeline: 988

When you call, text, or chat the 988 Lifeline, your conversation is confidential. Someone is available 24/7.

CopLine: 800-COPLINE (800-267-5463)

This resource is a confidential, 24-hour law enforcement officer hotline manned by retired law enforcement officers trained in active listening.

Crisis Text Line: Text BADGE to 741741 or call 800-273-TALK (800-273-8255)

A global organization providing free and confidential text-based mental health support 27/7 throughout the U.S., Canada, the U.K., and Ireland.

Code 4 Northwest: 425-243-5092

A crisis response and referral network for Washington state active and retired first responders, EMS, corrections, civilian support personnel, and their families. Free and confidential help, 24/7.

Frontline Helpline: 866-676-7500

Run by Frontline Responder Services. Offers 24/7 coverage with first-responder call-takers.

IAFF Firefighter/Family Crisis & Support Line: 844-525-FIRE (844-525-3473)

A 24/7 hotline for firefighters and family members to speak with mental health counselors who are trained in fire service culture.

Free Companion Materials

YOUR DOWNLOADABLE
PEER SUPPORT RESOURCES
for *Cover My Six: The Playbook* are available here:

https://drleasullivan.systeme.io/the-playbook-companion

Login is required to access:

- Personal Crisis Preplan (PDF) - A step-by-step guide to securing backup before you need it.

- Chapter 22: How to Vet a Therapist (PDF) - An excerpt from Cover My Six: A Comprehensive Guide to Firefighter Care to help you spot true cultural competence.

- Hold the Line (Audio Exercise) - A quick grounding tool for when you're on the go.

Log in, grab your tools, and put them to work—they're here to support you as you support your crews.

Free Newsletter

SIGN UP TODAY for Dr. Lea's free periodic newsletter here:

https://drleasullivan.systeme.io/newsletter

The *Cover My Six Newsletter* delivers real-world mental wellness strategies made for the fire service—no fluff, no lectures, just straight-up tools you can use on shift and at home. Designed by someone who understands the job. Backed by research. Tailored for the red line.

What You'll Get:

- Resources for emotional recovery

- Tactical tools for resilience

- Final Thought from Dr. Lea in each edition

And more!

There are many more support resources available
when you visit Dr. Lea's website:

https://DrLeaSullivan.com/

Including copies of her bestselling book *Cover My Six,* copies of *Cover My Six: The Playbook* (also available as a spiral-bound edition when purchased directly from the author), the audiobook edition of *Cover My Six,* and many free resources as well.

REFERENCES

[1] Horan, K. A., Marks, M., Ruiz, J., Bowers, C., & Cunningham, A. (2021). Here for my peer: The future of first responder mental health. *International Journal of Environmental Research and Public Health*, *18*(21), 11097. https://doi.org/10.3390/ijerph182111097

[2] Marks, M. R., Bowers, C., DePesa, N. S., Trachik, B., Deavers, F. E., & James, N. T. (2017). REACT: A paraprofessional training program for first responders-A pilot study. *Bulletin of the Menninger Clinic*, *81*(2), 150–166. https://doi.org/10.1521/bumc.2017.81.2.150

[3] Repper, J., & Carter, T. (2011). A review of the literature on peer support in mental health services. *Journal of Mental Health (Abingdon, England)*, *20*(4), 392–411. https://doi.org/10.3109/09638237.2011.583947

[4] Kleim, B. & Westphal, M. (2011). Mental health in first responders: A review and recommendation for prevention and intervention strategies. *Traumatology (Tallahassee, Fla.)*, *17*(4), 17–24. https://10.1177/1534765611429079

[5] Vigil, N. H., Grant, A. R., Perez, O., Blust, R. N., Chikani, V., Vadeboncoeur, T. F., Spaite, D. W., & Bobrow, B. J. (2019). Death by suicide—The EMS profession compared to the general public. *Prehospital emergency care*, *23*(3), 340–345. https://doi.org/10.1080/10903127.2018.1514090

[6] U.S. Department of Health & Human Services. (2024). The HIPAA Privacy Rule. Created September 27, 2024. Retried from https://www.hhs.gov/hipaa/for-professionals/privacy/index.html

[7] Social Work Institute. (2024). Confidentiality in counselling: Balancing trust and accountability. Created May 27, 2024. Retrieved from https://socialwork.institute/counselling-basics/confidentiality-in-counselling/

[8] Revised Code of Washington § 5.60.060(6). (n.d.). Who may not testify—Privileged communications. Washington State Legislature. Retrieved August 4, 2025, from https://app.leg.wa.gov/RCW/default.aspx?cite=5.60.060

[9] North Carolina General Statutes § 8–53.10. (n.d.). Peer support group counselors. Retrieved August 4, 2025, from https://www.ncleg.gov/EnactedLegislation/Statutes/HTML/BySection/Chapter_8/GS_8-53.10.html

[10] Mississippi Code § 13-1-22.1. (2013). Peer support communication privilege. Retrieved August 4, 2025, from https://law.justia.com/codes/mississippi/2013/title-13/chapter-1/in-general/section-13-1-22.1/

[11] Bowlby, J. (1982). *Attachment and loss: Volume I*. Attachment (2nd ed.). Basic Books.

[12] Landen, S. M., & Wang, C. C. D. C. (2010). Adult attachment, work cohesion, coping, and psychological well-being of firefighters. *Counselling Psychology Quarterly, 23*(2), 143–162. https://doi.org/10.1080/09515071003776028

[13] Ainsworth M. D., & Bell, S. M. (1970). Attachment, exploration, and separation: Illustrated by the behavior of one-year-olds in a strange situation. *Child Development, 41*(1), 49-67.

[14] Coan, J. A., Schaefer, H. S., & Davidson, R. J. (2006). Lending a hand: Social regulation of the neural response to threat. *Psychological Science, 17*(12), 1032–1039. https://doi.org/10.1111/j.1467-9280.2006.01832.x

[15] Bowlby, J. (1969). *Attachment. Attachment and loss: Vol. 1. Loss.* New York: Basic Books.

[16] Bowlby, J. (1982). *Attachment and loss: Volume I*. Attachment (2nd ed.). Basic Books.

[17] Mikulincer, M., & Shaver, P. R. (2007). *Attachment in adulthood: Structure, dynamics, and change*. The Guilford Press.

[18] Johnson, S. (2019). *Attachment theory in practice: Emotionally focused therapy with individuals, couples, and families*. The Guilford Press.

[19] Nakamura, Y., Lipschitz, D. L., Landward, R., Kuhn, R., & West, G. (2011). Two sessions of sleep-focused mind-body bridging improve self-reported symptoms of sleep and PTSD in veterans: A pilot randomized controlled trial. *Journal of psychosomatic research, 70*(4), 335–345. https://doi.org/10.1016/j.jpsychores.2010.09.007

[20] American Foundation for Suicide Prevention. (n.d.). Risk factors, protective factors, and warning signs. Retrieved on December 11, 2024, from https://afsp.org/risk-factors-protective-factors-and-warning-signs/#warning-signs

[21] World Health Organization. (2016). *Practice manual for establishing and maintaining surveillance systems for suicide attempts and self-harm.* WHO Press.

[22] Seattle Children's Research Hospital. (n.d.). Prevent Suicide: Ask the Question. Mental Health Resource Hub. Retrieved from https://www.seattlechildrens.org/health-safety/mental-health-resources/preventing-suicide/?utm_source=chatgpt.com

[23] Ramar, K., Malhotra, R. K., Carden, K. A., Martin, J. L., Abbasi-Feinberg, F., Aurora, R. N., Kapur, V. K., Olson, E. J., Rosen, C. L., Rowley, J. A., Shelgikar, A. V., Trotti, L. M. (2021). Sleep is essential to health: An American Academy of Sleep Medicine position statement. *Journal of Clinical Sleep Medicine, 7*(10):2115–2119. https://doi.org/10.5664/jcsm.9476

[24] Barnes, C. M., & Drake, C. L. (2015). Prioritizing sleep health: Public health policy recommendations. *Perspectives on Psychological Science, 10*(6), 733–737. https://doi.org/10.1177/1745691615598509

[25] James, S., Honn, K., Gaddameedhi, S., & Van Dongen, H. P. A. (2017). Shift work: Disrupted circadian rhythms and sleep—implications for health and well-being. *Current Sleep Medicine Reports.* In Press. https://doi.org/10.1007/s40675-017-0071-6.

[26] Frost, C., Toczko, M., Merrigan, J. J., & Martin, J. R. (2021). The effects of sleep on firefighter occupational performance and health: A systematic review and call for action. *Sleep Epidemiology, 12*(1). https://doi.org/10.1016/j.sleepe.2021.100014

[27] Luyster, F. S., Strollo, P. J., Jr, Zee, P. C., Walsh, J. K., & Boards of Directors of the American Academy of Sleep Medicine and the Sleep Research Society. (2012). Sleep: A health imperative. *Sleep, 35*(6), 727–734. https://doi.org/10.5665/sleep.1846

[28] Datta, K., Tripathi, M., Verma, M., Masiwal, D., & Mallick, H. N. (2021). Yoga nidra practice shows improvement in sleep in patients with chronic insomnia: A randomized controlled trial. *The National medical journal of India, 34*(3), 143–150. https://doi.org/10.25259/NMJI_63_19

[29] Caplin, A., Chen, F. S., Beauchamp, M. R., & Puterman, E. (2021). The effects of exercise intensity on the cortisol response to a subsequent acute psychosocial stressor. *Psychoneuroendocrinology, 131,* 105336. https://doi.org/10.1016/j.psyneuen.2021.105336

[30] Brooks, J., Fairbairn, P., Mantzouratou, A., Chester, L., & Tsofliou, F. (2024). The effect of healthy dietary patterns on stress, mood, and mental health outcomes: A systematic review. *Proceedings of the Nutrition Society, 83*(OCE4), E281. doi:10.1017/S0029665124005196

[31] Long, S. J., & Benton, D. (2013). Effects of vitamin and mineral supplementation on stress, mild psychiatric symptoms, and mood in nonclinical samples: A meta-analysis. *Psychosomatic medicine, 75*(2), 144–153. https://doi.org/10.1097/PSY.0b013e31827d5fbd

[32] Cain, T., Brinsley, J., Bennett, H., Nelson, M., Maher, C., & Singh, B.(2025). Effects of cold-water immersion on health and wellbeing: A systematic review and meta-analysis. *PLoS ONE 20*(1): e0317615. https://doi.org/10.1371/journal.pone.0317615

[33] Teległów, A., Wrześniewski, K., & Blecharz, J. (2025). Hormonal and psychological responses to a single cold-water immersion in regularly winter-swimming males. *Applied Sciences, 15*(13), 7107. https://doi.org/10.3390/app15137107

[34] McDonald, M. A., Meckes, S. J., & Lancaster, C. L. (2021). Compassion for oneself and others protects the mental health of first responders. *Mindfulness, 12*(3), 659–671. https://doi.org/10.1007/s12671-020-01527-y

[35] Joyce, S., Shand, F., Lal, T. J., Mott, B., Bryant, R. A., & Harvey, S. B. (2019). Resilience@Work mindfulness program: Results from a cluster randomized controlled trial with first responders. *Journal of Medical Internet Research, 21*(2), e12894. https://doi.org/10.2196/12894